Abou

Tony was born in Nottingham ...ues the seeds
were sown for his love affair ...Greece during a holiday on the
island of Skiathos. Since then he has visited many of the islands of
the Ionian and Aegean seas, as well as the mainland of Greece.

His heart though lies on the small, unspoilt islands of the Aegean.
When in 2006, he had the opportunity of retiring from his business
consultancy, he and his partner Carol chose Thassos as their base
as UK ex-pats, selecting to live on the outskirts of Thassos Town,
known locally as Limenas.

As an author of business books, Tony had been aware after his
many years travelling within Greece that what was lacking for the
holidaymaker and general traveller was a comprehensive, honest
and accurate guide to each island in an easy to read book.

In 2006 he wrote a book on his adopted island home of Thassos,
which has become a benchmark for holiday guides, selling
extensively in Europe and the United States.

In 2007 he decided to write his second travel guide on the island of
Kos and a year later added a third book on Santorini. This, his
fourth travel guide, was first published in January 2013. He hopes
that in the years to come, his continuing travels will allow him to
write guides for more of the Greek islands that he loves.

Opposite: 'Rhodes Venus' attributed to the sculptor Doidalsas
1st century B.C. (*Rhodes Archaeological Museum*)

A-Z Guide to

Rhodes
including Symi

Tony Oswin

Contents:
The island, its history, what to see, where to go, eating out, entertainment, the best beaches, travel information and a host of tips and hints for the holidaymaker and traveller.

2020 Edition

Published January 1, 2020 by arima publishing
www.arimapublishing.com
10th edition

ISBN: 978-1-84549-758-3

DISCLAIMER
The contents of these materials are for general guidance only and are not
intended to apply in specific circumstances. As such, the contents of these
materials should not be relied on for the purpose of deciding to do, or
omitting to do anything, and you should always seek independent advice in
relation to any particular question or requirement you might have. Any
opinions set out in these materials are those of the author only, and unless
expressly stated otherwise, are not the opinions of the publisher. To the
fullest extent permitted by law, the publisher and Tony Oswin expressly
disclaims any and all liability and responsibility to any person, in respect of
the consequences of anything done, or omitted to be done, in reliance on
the contents of these materials.

arima publishing
ASK House, Northgate Avenue
Bury St Edmonds, Suffolk, IP32 6BB
t: (+44) 01284 700321
www.arimapublishing.com

To the memory of Bobi....our four-legged friend

Foreword

I have been visiting Greece for over thirty years and during that time I have fallen in love with the country, its people and most of all the Greek approach to life.

However, during my travels I always found it difficult to obtain island specific guide books, written in English and containing up to the minute information and advice. Too many times, I returned home from a visit to Greece, only to talk to someone who advised me of something to do or see that I had been unaware of.

After moving to Greece in 2006, I realised that I now had the time and opportunity to fulfil that need, starting with a guide book on my adopted home island of Thassos. This, my second book in the series, is aimed at helping you to get the most out of your time on the cosmopolitan island of Rhodes. I hope that you will find it helpful and informative, both in planning your holiday and during your stay.

Occasionally I have been asked why there are no photographs in the book? When I first set out to write my travel guides, one major objective was to make sure the books were accurate and with the latest information at an affordable price. To achieve this, the publication process I chose was POD (*Print on Demand*), whereby each book is printed at the time of order, from a manuscript that is regularly updated. However, one drawback of POD is that at present, the addition of colour photographs adds considerably to the cost of each book.

As is the practice with books containing photographs, if they are to be offered at a reasonable price, they are printed in bulk to reduce the unit cost. This inevitably means that at these quantities, the book can be significantly out of date when purchased.

I hope you therefore agree that my decision to move all the media to the supporting website, so as to offer you both the highest quality and ensure the accuracy of information in the book, was the correct one.

As both official and local organisations have a habit of not releasing tourist related news, or information on tourist events until a few days before they start, I strongly recommend that you visit the website regularly whilst on the island. The latest news from the island is updated throughout each day to keep you constantly informed.

I wish you a wonderful 2020 holiday,

Tony Oswin

Our website can be found at:-

www.atoz-guides.com

(your password can be found on the 'Acknowledgements' page)

Our email address is:-

info@atoz-guides.com

A to Z Travel Club

Unique amongst travel guides, the 'A to Z' guides are designed in two parts. The printed book, which contains all the information you need on your travels around the island and the 'A to Z' website, which offers a wealth of supporting information. The website also allows us to bring you the very latest tourist news from the island, special 'members' offers and more high quality photographs and videos than with any other travel guide, including over 80 photographs, both 2D and 3D, aerial shots, panoramas, videos and webcams on the island.

All this is totally free to you and is accessed via a member's password. You will find your member password at the bottom of the 'Acknowledgements' page at the back of this book.

To access the full member benefits of the website, place your cursor over the 'Travel Club' button at the top of any website page. Next move your cursor down over 'Travel Club Rhodes' and a further drop down menu appears, then place your cursor over the desired page and click:-

Rhodes News - Tourist news updated throughout each day

Holiday Advice - A wide range of holiday related advice

Discounts & Offers - Holiday ideas and money saving offers

2D Gallery - Over 50 high quality 2D photographs and videos

Real 3D Gallery - Over 40 high quality 3D photos & panoramas

Rhodes Weather - Real-time weather and an 8 day forecast

Rhodes Travel Info - Flight information, money matters etc.

Rhodes Maps & Panoramas - Print-off maps and panoramas

Rhodes Links - Webcams and a wide range of Rhodes websites

www.atoz-guides.com

Contents

Rhodes

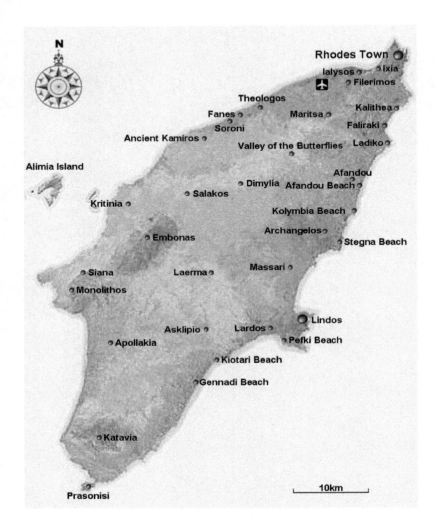

Due to the small size of the book, we are unable to include a more detailed map. However, if you visit our website there are maps of the island to download and print-off. Alternatively there are free maps available from most car hire companies and many other businesses once you are on the island.

The magical island of Rhodes

Rhodes (*Greek: Ρόδος, Ródos*) is an island in the Dodecanese chain, 77km by 34km at its widest points and only 18km from the coast of Turkey. The island covers an area of some 1,400 square kilometres, with its principal peak being Mount Attavyros, situated in the west of the central highlands and rising to a height of 1,216 metres.

Rhodes is the largest of the Dodecanese islands in terms of both land area and population, which at the last census numbered 120,000 inhabitants. The island lies in the centre of the Dodecanese chain and serves as its capital. The name Dodecanese is derived from the Greek word for *twelve islands*, which since additions after the Second World War, now actually comprises fourteen islands. These are Rhodes, Kos, Symi, Megisiti, Lipsoi, Telos, Astypalia, Kalymnos, Karpathos, Kasos, Leros, Nisyros, Patmos and Halki.

The principal town on the island is Rhodes, which comprises the Old and New towns numbering 54,000 residents in total. It is located at the far northern tip of the island, opposite the Turkish mainland. The Old Town is one of the best preserved medieval towns in Europe and has been declared a World Heritage Site.

Lindos is the second largest town, famous for its picturesque brilliant white painted architecture, its winding cobbled streets and the acropolis which towers over the town.

There are 44 villages on the island, the main ones being Faliraki, Archangelos, Monolithos, Ialysos, Maritsa, Siana, Afandou, Fanes and Massari.

The island is most famous for being the site of one of the "Seven Wonders of the Ancient World", the Colossus of Rhodes, which is often depicted as straddling the entrance to ancient Rhodes harbour. However, recent research has concluded that the 30 metre bronze statue depicting Helios, the Greek god of the sun, was more likely constructed on a plinth near to the harbour.

Today, Rhodes is one of the most popular tourist destinations in Europe, attracting over 2 million visitors in 2019, with the UK contributing approximately 380,000 to this figure. Sadly though, tourism has had a detrimental effect on the architecture and environment. It has also been a major factor in the diminishing role of traditional Greek culture on the island.

Rhodes offers the visitor both the opportunity to relax on the many beautiful beaches, as well as the chance to explore the island's long and fascinating history at the many archaeological sites, both in Rhodes Town and around the island.

The island's airport, Diagoras is one of the largest and busiest in Greece and connects the island with the other major Greek cities and islands as well as with major European capitals and cities via both charter and scheduled flights.

Rhodes is a major stopping off point for Aegean and Eastern Mediterranean cruises. So in the mornings, Akantia Harbour, the main port in Rhodes Town, swarms with passengers disembarking from at least one cruise ship that has docked for a day of sightseeing.

History

Prehistoric period (*pre 800 B.C.*)

Rhodes was inhabited in the Neolithic period (*New Stone Age*) as testified by recent discoveries of pottery and other artefacts in the Cave of Kalamonias, near the village of Kalithia and Koumelo Cave near Archangelos. Analysis of the finds, date the occupation of the caves to the 6/5th millennia B.C.

In Koumelo Cave, the stratified Neolithic remains in the cave were found under a deep layer of volcanic ash, which has been analysed and found to be from the 1627 B.C. mega volcanic eruption on the island of Santorini, known as the Minoan Eruption.

The Minoans (*a modern name, as no evidence has been found of their real name*) colonised Crete and many other Aegean islands including Santorini. Evidence confirms that they visited Rhodes if not colonised it. Later Rhodian mythology recall a story of a race on the island called the Telchines, who were known as excellent metallurgists in bronze and iron. It is interesting that the Telchines are also associated with the story of Atlantis and that we know from archaeological finds on Santorini and Crete that the Minoans were equally skilled in metallurgy. More and more evidence is coming to light to link Santorini with the fabled Atlantis, so could it be that the Telchines were the same race that populated the fabled Atlantis and that today we call the Minoans?

In the aftermath of the 1627 eruption on Santorini, the Minoan civilisation declined and in the 15th century, the "new kids on the block", the Mycenaean Greeks, from the city-state of Mycenae in the Peloponnese, invaded and colonized Rhodes.

During the 12th century, Mycenaean dominance of the Aegean region collapsed and Greece entered what is referred to as "The Dark Ages". This was a period when most civilisations in the Mediterranean and Middle East either collapsed, or disappeared from the records completely (*ca. 1200-800 BC*). The reason for this upheaval is still unclear, but has been associated with an influx of a warrior race, referred to by the Egyptians of the time as the "Sea Peoples".

Archaic period (*800-480 B.C.*)

In the 8th century, Greece emerges from The Dark Ages and on Rhodes there is evidence that the Dorians, a race from the mainland of Greece settled the island, founding a number of important settlements, including the cities of Ialysos, Kameiros and Lindos. The Dorians also established cities on Kos, at Cnidus and Halicarnassus (*modern day Bodrum in Turkey*), creating what was known as the Dorian Hexapolis (*meaning six cities*).

In the latter half of the 8th century, contacts with other civilisations in the Mediterranean area seem to have flourished as did trade, confirmed by artefacts from Cyprus, Syria and the Middle East, found at a number of sites on the island. Trading links were also developed with the Phoenicians, especially from the city of Ialysos.

In the following centuries Rhodes competed with the mainland city state of Corinth for control of the lucrative trading markets in the Eastern Mediterranean, especially in ceramics. Cereals were an important import from Egypt and therefore the island maintained a significant presence in Naukratis, a Greek trading post on the Nile Delta. It was also at this time that the Rhodians founded colonies across the Mediterranean, as far afield as the Balearic Isles and Spain.

During the late 6th and early 5th centuries, the Persian Empire was on the ascendancy and in 491/490 the Persians unsuccessfully laid siege to Lindos. However, when the Persians returned in 481 in greater strength, the islanders were forced to join the Persians in their assault against Athens and the other Greek city-states.

The Persian navy was defeated by the Greek alliance at the Battle of Salamis near Athens in 480 and in the following year their army was defeated at the Battle of Plataea, north of Athens. The Persians withdrew from mainland Greece and in 478, a naval force, sent from Athens, defeated the Persian occupiers on Rhodes.

Animosity between the Greek city-states of Athens and Sparta as to which was the more powerful had always existed, but with the

Persian threat resolved, the two city-states now started forming alliances and enrolling like-minded city-states into their respective confederacies. Rhodes, as principally a naval power sided with Athens and joined their confederacy, known as the 'Athenian League'.

Classical period *(480-323 B.C.)*

When the Peloponnesian War broke out between Athens and Sparta and their respective leagues in 431, Rhodes remained largely neutral, although it continued to be a member of the Athenian League. The war dragged on until 404, in which year Sparta and its allies finally defeated Athens. However, by this time Rhodes had seen "the writing on the wall" and in 412 they withdrew entirely from the conflict and left the Athenian League to pursue an independent future.

In 408, the island's cities united to form one overall and more powerful city-state. It was at this time that the city of Rhodes was founded in its present position to act as a new capital.

The Peloponnesian War had resulted in the subjugation of Athens by Sparta, but in the following decades Sparta itself declined as a military force. This left Greece and the Aegean islands politically fragmented and vulnerable and in 357, Mausolos, the King of Caria (*a state in present day Turkey*) attacked and occupied Rhodes. However, seventeen years later, the Persians defeated Caria and in turn took Rhodes as a prize. Their acquisition of the island only lasted until 332, when during the epic campaign of Alexander the Great against the Persians, Alexander's forces liberated the island, returning it to full independence.

Hellenistic period *(323-31 B.C.)*

Alexander had not named a successor, so on his death in 323, his generals carved up the empire between them. Ptolemy took Egypt, Seleucus took the eastern part of the empire and Antigonus took Asia Minor and the north of what is now Syria.

Due to their existing strong trading ties with Egypt, Rhodes, both from loyalty and an eye on their future prosperity, saw Egypt and the Ptolemies as their closest allies, and so the Rhodo-Egyptian alliance was established with the aim of developing and controlling trade throughout the Aegean region. Prosperity did follow, with the island developing into a strong maritime trading centre, as can be testified by Rhodian coinage found in archaeological digs throughout the Mediterranean region.

As was the case throughout the Hellenistic world, art, science, philosophy and astronomy flourished on Rhodes, with many famous figures either being of Rhodian birth, or choosing to reside on what was seen to be an influential and progressive island. These included, Apollonius of Rhodes, Eudemus of Rhodes, Chares of Lindos (*the sculptor of the "Colossus of Rhodes"*) and Athenian rhetorician, Aeschines, who created a school on Rhodes.

Antagonism and rivalry between Alexander's ex-generals had persisted ever since his death. Antigonus, who had desires on Ptolomy's Egypt, realised that he first needed to take Egypt's ally Rhodes. So in 305, he sent his army, commanded by his son Demetrius, to besiege the island. Demetrius had already built a reputation as a great general, being known to his contemporaries as "The Besieger".

The siege of Rhodes is famous for two reasons. First, for the huge size of the besieging force and the massive siege-engines employed (*one siege-tower called Helepolis weighed in at a staggering 163 tons [148,000 kg]*), but after a year without success in breaching the city's strong defensive walls, Demetrius left the island. The second is, that after Demetrius' departure, the Rhodians sold the siege equipment left behind and with the 300 talents received (*equivalent to 4 million euro today*), they commissioned the "Colossus of Rhodes" to celebrate the victory, which was erected between 292 and 280. This statue of the sun god Helios, stood over 30 metres tall and was constructed of an iron frame plated in bronze, today it is known as one of the "Seven Wonders of the Ancient World".

What followed was 150 years of increased economic and political power for Rhodes. The island continued to control the grain trade in the eastern Mediterranean and to secure their dominance, they built one of the largest and finest navies of the time. After the decline of the power of the Ptolemies in Egypt in the latter years of the 3rd century, Rhodes became the prime trading nation and port in the eastern Mediterranean. In the financial world of the time it was also seen as powerful, with private banks that loaned money to other Greek city-states.

Rhodes even managed to derive advantage from the terrible earthquake of 226/227 that destroyed large parts of the capital and toppled the Colossus of Rhodes. While 226 is most often cited as the date of the quake, sources variously cite 226 or 227 as the date when it occurred.

In the aftermath, most other Greek city states sent financial help, allowing the Rhodians to re-construct the city, even more impressive in its design and extent than before, although the Colossus was never re-built. The remnants of the statue lay in place for nearly eight centuries before being sold off by invaders.

However, the expansionist aims of the Antigonid Empire had never diminished and in 201, threatened once again by Macedonian aggression, Rhodes was forced to turn for help from the new emerging political and military power in the Mediterranean, Rome.

Although weakened by a 17 year-long war against Hannibal and Carthage, Rome saw Rhodes as important in her long term political and economic plans and offered military help. The result was the Second Macedonian War (*200-196*), which ended Macedon's role as a major political player and preserved Rhodian independence.

Rhodes and Rome now became allies and in gratitude to Rhodes for their help in the war against the Seleucid Empire, Rome's senate ceded large tracts of land in eastern Anatolia (*modern day Turkey*) to Rhodes, further extending her influence and power in the region.

However, Rome withdrew its forces from the east, as the senate saw client-kingdoms as preferable to keeping a costly military presence in the area. It was clear that Rome was the dominant force in the known world and Rhodian independence was ultimately dependent upon good relations with them.

In 164, Rhodes was finally annexed by Rome in all but name, ending an independence that was no longer sustainable. It was said that the Romans ultimately turned against their former ally because the Rhodians were the only people they had encountered who were more arrogant than themselves!

After the murder of Julius Caesar in 44 B.C., the senate exiled Cassius, one the conspirators, to the eastern provinces. Cassius set about building an army and sought help from Rhodes, but as this was not forthcoming, he attacked the island and sacked the city.

In year 57 A.D., Saint Paul visited Rhodes on his 3rd missionary journey, staying as most believe in Lindos, but there are no records of him preaching on the island. Christianity didn't take route on the island until the late 4th century, but subsequently became an important centre for the new religion in the eastern Aegean.

In 142, another major earthquake devastated the island, but despite all the assistance from Rome, Rhodes never recovered and became just one of many provincial cities in the vast Roman Empire. It was seen by successive Emperors as a favourite place of exile for political enemies.

Medieval period (*500-1500 A.D.*)

During the early Christian period (*330-650*) Rhodes belonged to the eastern part of the Christianised Eastern Roman Empire, which is known in history as the Byzantine Empire.

A serious earthquake in 515 once again destroyed much of the city. The city was re-built by its Byzantine rulers, but to a smaller scale, only covering the area which now comprises Rhodes Old Town.

The new city was divided into two main quarters, the Acropolis (*later the site for the Palace of the Grand Master*), and the Polis (*lower town*).

In the 7th century, Rhodes became a target for pirate raids, resulting in the town's fortifications being strengthened, but to no avail, as in 653 the island was attacked and captured by Arab forces who sacked the island, including taking away the remnants of the Colossus of Rhodes. In 715, the Byzantine Empire initiated a rebellion on Rhodes, which led to the expulsion of the Arabs and the installation once again of Byzantine rule, which continued almost unbroken for the next 500 years.

As Byzantine power declined in the 13th century the island was first occupied by the Genoese, but in 1309 after the final collapse of the Byzantine Empire, the Order of the Hospitaller Knights of St. John of Jerusalem settled on the island. This was to be their new headquarters in Europe, from where they could offer a safe haven for pilgrims travelling to Jerusalem and the Holy Land.

The Hospitallers rebuilt the city as a model of a European ideal. Many of the city's famous and magnificent monuments, including the Palace of the Grand Master, were built during this period. The city's fortifications were massively strengthened, incorporating sections of the Byzantine walls, but enclosing a larger area than the previous Byzantine town. The north quarter, the Collachium, was set aside as the administrative centre, containing amongst other official buildings, the Palace of the Grand Master, the Hospital and the 'Inns' for the various nationalities of knights. The larger, south quarter, called the Burgum, became the residential and trading centre of the new city.

The immense fortifications you see today withstood many attacks in the next two centuries from those who continually viewed Rhodes as strategically important and a great prize. These included an attack by the Sultan of Egypt in 1444 and a siege by the Ottoman ruler Mehmed II in 1480. However, in 1522, The Knights finally capitulated http://en.wikipedia.org/wiki/Siege_of_Rhodes_(1522)to Suleiman the Magnificent, who besieged the town with an army of

100,000. Although none of these attacks ever managed to breech the walls, their ferocity can be testified to by the vast number of stone mortar balls that litter the town. If you go to the Gate of Eleftherias and walk down through the car park to the sea, on your right around 100 metres down that section of defensive wall you will see one mortar ball that hit with such force that it 'melted' into the solid stone fortifications.

Suleiman was gracious in his victory and allowed the few Knights that were left to leave the castle unharmed and sail to a new base in Sicily, although they later moved their headquarters to Malta.

For the next four hundred years, Rhodes was ruled by the leaders of the Ottoman Empire who built many the mosques, libraries and baths (*Hamams*).

Modern history

Rhodes fell to the Italians in 1912 during the Italo-Turkish War. With the signing of the 'Treaty of Lausanne', which officially ended the war between Turkey and the alliance of England, France, Italy, Greece and the Balkan states, Rhodes along with the other Dodecanese islands were ceded to Italy.

In 1929 the Italian administration declared the medieval walls and cemeteries of Rhodes Old Town historic monuments. Ottoman additions were dismantled and the fortifications and walls were restored. The Palace of the Grand Master was rebuilt and the Street of the Knights was reconstructed to its former glory.

Italy occupied Rhodes until September 1943, when after the downfall of Mussolini, they switched sides to the allies. Germany fearing the allies would seize this strategically positioned island, swiftly dispatched forces. With the German occupation of the island secure, in July the following year, the Gestapo started deporting all the Jewish community to Auschwitz. Out of a total of 2,000 Jews on the island before the Second World War, only an estimated 160 survived the conflict. In Rhodes Old Town, in rooms adjacent to the Kahal Shalom synagogue, there is a Jewish museum that records the history of the Jewish community on Rhodes before the Second

World War. The museum is open in the summer months from 10:00 until 15:00, closed on Saturdays.

In 1948, together with the other islands of the Dodecanese, Rhodes was united with the rest of Greece. After 1960, Rhodes Old Town was declared a monument of cultural heritage by the Greek Ministry of Culture and in 1988 the medieval city was added to the UNESCO World Heritage List.

Mythology

There are many conflicting myths regarding Rhodes that have been recorded during the centuries. One ancient myth describes a sea-nymph called Rhode who was goddess of the island.

She was said to be the daughter of Poseidon and Halia. Pindar (*ca. 522–443 B.C.*) a famous Greek poet, declares that the island was said to be born of the union of Helios the sun god and the nymph Rhode. She was with Helios one of the protectors of the island, which was the sole centre of her cult. Her name was applied to the rose, which appeared on ancient Rhodian coinage. Rhoda is also the name of a pink hibiscus plant, which is native to the island.

The myth goes on to say that three of the sons of Helios and Rhode were Ialysos, Kamiros and LIndos. Hellios divided the island equally between his sons, who each built a citadel and from whence the modern-day place names are derived.

Diodorus Siculus a writer of the 1st century B.C., proclaimed that Actis, one of the other sons of Helios and Rhode, travelled to Egypt, where he built the great city of Heliopolis and taught the Egyptians the science of astrology.

Colossus of Rhodes

There are theories that the Colossus was never located in the port, but rather was part of the Acropolis of Rhodes on the hill today named Monte Smith, which overlooks the port area. The temple on top of Monte Smith is traditionally thought to have been devoted to

Apollo, but according to some, it was a sanctuary to Helios. The enormous stone foundations at the temple site, the function of which is not definitively known by modern scholars, are proposed to have been the supporting platform of the Colossus.

The fortress of St Nicholas is also proposed as the location. The fort's floor contains a large circle of sandstone blocks, which may have been the statue's foundation. Curved and finely cut blocks of marble incorporated into the structure, may be the remains of a marble base that sat upon the sandstone foundation. However, we may never know the true location of the statue.

In December of 2015, a group of European architects announced plans to build a modern Colossus striding two piers at the harbour entrance, despite the preponderance of evidence and scholarly opinion that the original monument could not have been located there. The new statue, 150 metres tall (five times the height of the original) would cost an estimated 264 million euro, which would be funded by private donations. The plans included a cultural centre, a library, an exhibition hall, and a lighthouse, all powered by solar panels.

For those readers interested in ancient history, I have included a Time-Line at the back of the book. The events mentioned in the book are in bold.

Culture

For those who have not visited Greece before, how can I explain the Greek people and their culture? It could be said that their way of life reflects many of the positive attributes of the UK in the not so distant past. These include a greater reliance and respect within the community for the family as well as the individual, a belief that the quality of life is more important than the quantity and a stronger self-reliance, rather than an increasing dependence on the state.

All I will say is that I find the Greek islanders honest, sincere and extremely friendly and one of my greatest hopes is that the ever-increasing exposure to the tourist trade does not devalue, or corrupt these virtues.

You will find that, as in many Mediterranean countries, much of the day-to-day activities start very early, stop at lunchtime and reconvene early evening, continuing late into the night. So expect many of the shops and other services to be closed for a few hours in the afternoon. Remember the old adage "only mad dogs and Englishmen go out in the midday sun". I can confirm though there are no mad dogs. You will see a few that appear to be stray, but the majority have owners who let them out to wander free during the day. All in my experience are very friendly and pose no risk.

During your stay, one of the simplest ways of saying thank you (*Efkaristo*) is to take time to learn a few basic Greek words and phrases. I can assure you that even though the majority of Rhodians in the main tourist areas speak at least a little English, your attempt to speak their language, if only a few words, will be much appreciated. To that end, I have added a glossary of frequently used Greek words and phrases at the back of the book.

Beyond the tourist

With the first drops of rain another summer season comes to a close. The days get shorter and the sunsets are a deeper red and purple. The Meltemi winds (*the Aegean equivalent of the French Mistral*) strengthen in the evenings and there is a fresher feel in the air; reminding all on the island that winter is approaching.

The warm sunny weather continues for the whole of September and well into October. The first fall of leaves bring a new urgency, the tourists may be leaving, but this is a busy time for the islanders.

Many of the locals have two separate lives, the first during the holiday season, working in the many service industries dedicated to the tourist industry. Then, once the tourists have left, they return to one that is more reminiscent of the past life on the island, employed in more traditional trades such as agriculture, fishing and community services.

Winters on Rhodes are very mild, with temperatures dropping to an average of 12°C during January and February. Showers can be expected between October and May. December and January tend to be the wettest months, with rainfall decreasing dramatically after April. The sun continues to shine during the winter, with Rhodes still receiving an average of 5 to 6 hours a day.

Olive picking

The olive picking season usually starts in late October, but is dependent on the quality of the growing season. Most Rhodian families own some olive groves, which have been passed down through the generations. The men beat the olives down from the trees using long sticks (*or, more often nowadays, an electric beater*), whilst the women and children pick them up by hand off large nets that are spread under the olive trees. When the olives have been gathered, those not destined for eating whole, are taken to the olive press, where they are pressed to extract the olive oil.

The first oil of the season is the best and is used for salads, etc., whilst the old oil from the previous year is reserved for frying, or for lighting the icon lamps in the church.

Only in mid-December can the Rhodians slow down and start preparing for Christmas.

Religious festivals and cultural events

A large number of religious festivals and cultural events are staged by the Rhodians during the summer season. I have arranged them in month order to help you to easily identify those that are taking place during your holiday. Please note: The exact dates for some of the events are not confirmed until nearer to the event.

Information on most festivals and cultural events will be posted on the 'Rhodes News' page on our website.

April

Orthodox Easter Sunday – April 19th.

May

Lacania – 4/5th May, a major celebration for Aghia Irini.

Rhodes Town - The International Choir Festival and competition attracts choirs from all around the world and is held during the middle of May.

Rhodes Town - 26th May, the Anthestiria flower festival is an impressive parade with floats in Mandraki harbour.

June

All of Greece – 7/8th June, the major Festival of the Holy Spirit (*Pentecost*).

Lindos - 28th June, religious feast, Aghii Apostoli Monastery at Lindos.

July

Lindos - 6th July, a festival at Aghia Kyriaki Monastery in Kalathos.

Rhodes Town - During the first week of July there will be cultural events as part of the Maritime Week celebrations, with tours of Rhodes Town, free entry to museums, sports events, art exhibitions and firework displays.

Koskinou - 17th July, a major celebration for Aghia Marina.

Archangelos - 17th July, traditional feast of Aghia Marina.

Paradisi - 12th to 17th July, coincides with the feast day of Aghia Marina and will include dancing, concerts by the local philharmonic band and musical evenings.

Paradisi - 17th July, a wonderful religious feast at Aghia Marina.

Rhodes Town - 20 to 30th July, the International Opera Festival will take place in the courtyard of the Palace of the Grand Master.

Soroni - 23rd July for 10 days, this is the most famous celebration on the island. It is held at the Aghios Soulas Monastery and includes sports events, horse races and traditional music & dance.

Kattavia - 26th July, the feast of Aghia Paraskevi.

Rhodes Old Town - 27th July, the feast of Aghios Panteleimon.

August

Kiotari - A summer concert on Kiotari Beach is held each year in August.

Maritsa - 1st to 7th August, a festival including concerts, dance shows and theatrical performances.

Ialysos - events will be held in the first half of August with traditional dancing, sports events, concerts, choirs, art exhibitions and book fairs.

Kremista - 11th to 23rd August, the Kremasti Cultural Festival includes dancing, theatrical performances, musical evenings, concerts with choirs and the philharmonic band, beach parties, backgammon, draughts and chess competitions and tastings of the local cuisine.

Lindos - 14th August, a feast celebrating the Virgin Mary.

Afandou - 15th August, the Dormition of the Virgin, on the beach at Katholiki.

Kremista - 15th August, feast at the magnificent Church of the Dormition. This is one of the largest feasts on the island.

Embonas - 15th August, the feast of the Virgin Mary.

Ialysos - 15th August, Zoodochos Pigi Church. The icon of the Virgin will be paraded through the streets. Italian priests from Assisi take part in the celebration.

Archangelos - During the second half of August there will be a week of cultural events in the village of Archangelos with book fairs, talks and traditional dancing.

Lindos - 22nd August, a feast celebrating the Virgin Mary at Panaghia Ipseni Monastery.

Rhodes Town - 20 to 30th August, an International Dance Festival.

Archangelos - 23rd August, traditional feast of Panaghia Alemonitra (*Eleimonitria*).

Rhodes Old Town - 27th August, the feast of Aghios Fanourios.

September

Pastida - 1st to 7th September, festival celebrations in the village.

Kalithea - 13th to 15th September, a major celebration will be held as part of the feast of the Church of the Holy Cross. The celebration includes traditional music concerts.

Rhodes Town - "Days of Music" are classical concerts including music from all over the world. The venues are in Rhodes Old Town during September.

Rhodes - 27th September, World Tourism Day. The festival will be accompanied by traditional dancing, music groups, choirs from all over the Dodecanese. On the opening day there will be a firework display. Throughout the entire festival traditional Dodecanese delicacies will be on offer for visitors to try.

Afandou - 27th September, World Tourism Day will be celebrated with various events in Afandou and Kolymbia.

Kalithea - 27th September, World Tourism Day will be celebrated amid great festivity in all districts of the Municipality. There are music and dance events and at night firework displays.

Theologos - 27th September, World Tourism Day will be celebrated with a party which lasts four days in and around Theologos.

Archangelos - 8th September, a traditional feast with popular music at Panaghia Tsambika.

Damatria - 13th September, a major celebration will be held at Holy Cross Monastery (*Ipsosi Stavrou Monastery*).

Kritinia - 8th September at the Amartou Monastery, food and drink will be served accompanied by live traditional music.

Embonas - a wine festival with wine, grapes and must-jelly (an island delicacy) being served. This will be followed by traditional dancing. Held in the second half of September.

Local products

Ceramics

Rhodes has been associated with pottery and ceramic manufacturing since ancient times. In the 7th and 6th centuries B.C. Rhodes competed with the city-state of Corinth in producing Greece's finest pottery. You will see examples on display in the archaeological museum in Rhodes Old Town. The characteristic vivid coloured designs on ancient Rhodian pottery included wild goats, deer, griffins and pomegranate flowers, alternating with chains of anthemia and lotus blossoms.

Sadly many of the island's pottery factories have closed as fashions have changed, with those that still survive resorting to the production of hand painted souvenir items, typically vases, plates and ash trays, or reproductions of ancient pottery, which still have a market with the island's tourists.

Embroidery and carpets

Rhodes is also famous for its hand-woven carpets and rugs called Kilims. Kilims originated in ancient Persia and were introduced to the island during the Ottoman occupation. They are still hand-made in Afandou, Archangelos and Lindos.

You will see lace and beautiful multicoloured embroideries being sold by the womenfolk in many of the villages and on the climb up to Acropolis in Lindos.

Insider tip: Similar products are nowadays shipped in from Asia, so you might be better off asking for local help to confirm the best places to shop for the 'real' item!

Honey

As you drive round the island you are sure to notice colourful painted beehives especially in the more rural parts of the island and forested areas.

Honey is the most ancient Greek sweetener, with some of the best Greek honey being produced on Rhodes, helped by the unremitting sunshine and the abundance of flowing plants throughout the summer months.

Most sweets in Greece contain honey, from honey cakes, dough fritters drizzled with honey, cheese pies laced with honey, honey-sesame confectionary, to fruits and nuts preserved in honey.

It is a perfect gift to take back home and if you live in the EU, there are no Customs restrictions on this product.

Olives

Greece is the third largest producer of olive oil in the world, with the majority of the oil produced being of the highest quality of 'Extra Virgin'.

The Greeks actually consume more olive oil per person than any other country in the world as it is seen as an indispensable part of Greek cooking and an important contribution to a healthy diet. Olive oil is a mono-saturated fatty acid, which does not have the same cholesterol-raising effect of saturated fats as well as being a good source of antioxidants.

As well as its use in cooking, olive oil has many uses in industry and as a traditional fuel for lamps, as you will see in many of the island's churches.

The olive harvest begins in October for table olives and continues for about two months, depending on the weather, the type of olive and the conditions in which it is cultivated.

Insider tip: *The bags of olives sold in some supermarkets can be quite salty for some people's taste, so it may be better opting for the variety in jars.*

To confirm the different grades, Extra Virgin olive oil comes from a production that is traditional and includes no chemical processes.

The oil has no more than 0.8% acidity, and is judged to have a superior taste. It is used on salads, added at the table to food and for dipping.

Virgin olive oil comes from the same production process as Extra Virgin oil, but has an acidity less than 1.5%, and is judged to have a good taste.

Bottles labelled as "Pure olive oil" or "Olive oil" are usually a blend of refined and virgin production oil.

Wine

Since ancient times Rhodes has been famous for its wines. The present day wineries are centred around the village of Embonas.

Embonas has excellent conditions for grape cultivation and during harvest time the village streets are filled with baskets of grapes, as they wait to be spread out in the yards to dry in the sun before the main processing begins.

One of the largest wineries is Emery, which offer guided tours and the opportunity to purchase a bottle or two to take home (*if it makes it that far*). Three smaller traditional wineries in the village are, Alexandris, Kounakis and Merkouris.

The most famous wines of Rhodes are "Ilios" and "Grand Maitre" which are dry white wines and "Chevalier de Rhodes" which is a dry red wine.

Local domesticated animals

Cattle
Cattle are bred on the island for their meat and milk with the majority of livestock farms situated in the coastal areas such as the village of Kalavarda, near Kamiros.

Dogs and cats

There are large numbers of cats on the island (*most seem to be feral*) and a few dogs wandering free. The majority of the dogs have owners, but they are allowed to wander free during the day. Whether part feral or owned, the dogs are very friendly and pose no problem, except that is for taverna staff who tend to chase them off for the sake of their diners.

Rhodian Miniature Horses *(see page 65)*

The Rhodian Horse (*Equus caballus*) is one of the smallest horses in the world. Domesticated, their use declined in the last century due to farm mechanisation, leading to them being released and left to fend for themselves in the forests around Archangelos. This has resulted in a dramatic collapse of their population and sadly left the species on the edge of extinction.

Poultry

Free-range chickens are reared on the island and one thing I can say, having been used to factory-farmed varieties in the UK, is that they taste wonderful, especially when they are cooked on a rotisserie with olive oil and herbs.

Sheep and goats

Whilst sheep and goat rearing is not a prime farming activity on Rhodes, on your travels you will see large numbers, especially goats, as the resulting meat and milk is an important addition to the islands food production, such as in the making of Feta cheese.

Wildlife

For those interested in wildlife (*the animal type*), I have added the following information:

Birds

The best areas for bird-watching are in the Apolakkia dam area, Ialysos, Kalithea, Ixia, Kremasti Bridge and Koskinou. Ataviros and Profitis Ilias are well known for sightings of vultures, hawks, Peregrine falcons, kestrels, eagles including the Golden Eagle and owls (*their calls are a familiar sound during the night*).

The species that can be found on Rhodes include the Collared Dove, Blue Tit, Crested Lark, Sardinian Warbler and House Sparrow (*which you will find are very tame*) but, there have also been reports of rarer species such as Baillon's Crakes, Short-toed Larks, White-tailed Lapwing, Trumpeter Finch and Black-headed Bunting.

Other species include Cretzschmar's Bunting, Golden Oriole, Audouin's Gull, Calandra lark, Lanner Falcon, Long-Legged Buzzard and White-winged Black Tern. Sightings of Bonelli's Eagle, an endangered species, has also been reported.

Dolphins

Although dolphins are to be found in the whole of the Mediterranean, they are a rare sight in open waters. However, in 2011 pods were seen a number of times from the tourist boats. So keep an eye out, you may just be lucky.

Fallow Deer

The island is home to a population of wild fallow deer. One of the best places to see them is in Rodini Park, in the suburbs of Rhodes Town, where there is a herd of about 80 (*see page 42*). The Rhodian fallow deer is smaller than those found in central and northern Europe, though they are similarly coloured. Genetic testing in 2005 confirmed that the Rhodian fallow deer was distinct from all other populations and action was called for to both conserve the remaining stock and implement a long-term breeding programme.

It is the fallow deer that is portrayed as the island's emblem on the columns at the entrance to Mandraki Harbour.

Hummingbird?

You may see during your visit, a tiny flying creature that can easily be mistaken for a Hummingbird. In fact, this will most likely be a Hummingbird Moth, which is native to the island. Sadly Hummingbirds are only found in the New World.

Other mammals

Apart from the odd feral goat and cat, wild mammals are scarce and inconspicuous on the island. Especially at night, the occasional brown rat can be seen scurrying across the road, or scavenging near to waste bins. At dusk, bats can be seen swooping through the evening sky feeding on the myriad of insects. The occasional dead hedgehog on the road, especially in the north, bares testament to their presence and in addition, stone martens and brown hares have also been seen on the island.

Greece reportedly supports ninety-five species of land mammals and research shows that Rhodes shares in this diversity. Research has identified a distribution of twenty-five species of rodent around Greece. However, just four species in total have been reported from the Aegean islands, namely the lesser mole rat, the broad-toothed field mouse, the brown rat and the house mouse.

Sponges

Look in any gift shop on Rhodes and it is almost certain you will see sponges for sale as souvenirs and it has to be remembered that these are the remains of a marine animal, not a plant. The nearby island of Kalymnos was once the sponge diving capital of the world.

Getting there

Package holidays

The first and obvious way of visiting Rhodes is by booking through a tour operator. The major UK companies that are offering holidays on Rhodes in 2020 are in alphabetical order:-

First Choice (parent company TUI)
Jet2.com
Olympic Holidays
TUI

A la Carte

Flight only

Most if not all of the major tour companies also offer flight-only alternatives and to give you an idea, the cost of a return flight from the UK into Rhodes Airport during the summer season, start from around £120 per person. The three main holiday companies that also offer flight-only are listed below:-

www.jet2.com

www.tui.co.uk

UK budget airlines with direct flights to Rhodes include easyJet, and Ryanair. The websites can be found at:-

www.easyJet.com

www.ryanair.com

Hotels, studios and apartments

As you can appreciate, there is a vast selection of holiday accommodation on the island, from the large hotel complexes in the main resorts to the charismatic boutique hotels in the historic Rhodes Old Town, such as 'In Camera Art Boutique Hotel', all the way down to basic studios. As you can appreciate, this means that to cover the vast array of hotels and studios on the island to suit all tastes, I would have to write a book just on accommodation.

My advice would be to first decide on the resort that suits your needs. As they say, one of the most important points is "location, location, location." If you want that quiet relaxing holiday, you don't want to be above a taverna and if you like the nightlife, you don't want to be in the middle of nowhere! Once you have decided on the resort you can search the web by entering, for example, *hotels in Rhodes Town*. There are a large number of hotel agency websites that offer the full range of accommodation on the island for you to choose from. Once you have your short-list, it is always advisable to check the hotels against review websites.

One point I believe is less important is for your accommodation to offer a restaurant service. One of the joys of Rhodes is to visit the vast choice of tavernas and restaurants on the island and enjoy what can invariably be attractive surroundings and good food. Who wants to frequent a hotel restaurant, when you can sit by the sea and watch the sun set over the Aegean. If you have a family, you will find that the Greek culture is very family orientated and therefore children are welcomed and catered for by restaurant staff. Most tavernas offer breakfast, either continental or English.

One thing I can confirm is that without exception, the accommodation I have stayed in within Greece in the last 30 years has always been clean and good value for money. You may find that at the budget end of the market, things can be a bit basic as far as room facilities are concerned. However, the top end of the market you can expect a high standard and at a reasonable price.

Most 'self-catering' apartments and studios will have at least a two-ring stove, a fridge and basic cutlery, pots and pans and utensils, a double or two single beds with side cupboards and a wardrobe. Usually there is only a shower with a W.C. For those who like a good night's sleep, it may be advisable if you are visiting in the high season, to select accommodation that has air-conditioning in the rooms. Telephones, televisions and hair-dryers are usually only found in the more expensive accommodation.

Insider tip: If you are not staying in 'self-catering' accommodation, many hotels and apartments have rules against meals being prepared and eaten in the rooms. I would also advise that where it is acceptable, it is courteous to dispose of any food waste yourself, and not to leave it for the hotel cleaning staff.

One strange but positive anomaly I have noticed in the past is that room cleaning and laundry changes occur more regularly than is specified in the brochure or room information. You should also find that when the odd problem such as a blocked sink or faulty light arises, raising the issue with the management will invariably result in a quick solution.

An alternative to booking from home is to take a flight to Rhodes and look for your accommodation when you arrive on the island. You will find there is always some accommodation available and at most times you can negotiate a good price. In Rhodes Town, as with the other main resorts, there are a number of travel agencies who may have suitable accommodation on their books, or at least will point you in the right direction.

Camping

For those who enjoy the "back to nature" style holiday, or are looking for a *budget* way of visiting Rhodes, I am afraid Rhodes is not for you. There used to be a campsite at Ladiko (*Faliraki Camping*), but that closed in 2003. It is also illegal to just pitch a tent anywhere, but there are a few suitable beaches in the south of the island, such as Glyfada and Prassonissi, but in my view the better option is to find a cheap B&B and stay legal.

Tony Oswin

Places of interest

I have refrained from giving a 'star rating' as some guide books do, as my experience from acting as a guide is that "a wonderful experience" to one person, can be "a bore" to another.

However to help, I have ranked below the top five historical and archaeological sites in order of visitor numbers.

1. **Rhodes medieval town, moat and fortifications (*pages 41/196*)**
2. **Acropolis of Lindos (*pages 57/201*)**
3. **Ancient Kamiros (*pages 55/200*)**
4. **Rhodes Town acropolis (*pages 43/198*)**
5. **Filerimos (*pages 56/199*)**

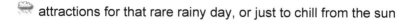 attractions for that rare rainy day, or just to chill from the sun

Insider tip: *If you are planning to explore Rhodes Old Town, wear a pair of comfortable walking shoes as the cobbled streets can play havoc with the soles of your feet.*

Insider tip: *You can save money by purchasing a special ticket from any of the museum ticket offices that covers in one ticket: The Palace of the Grand Masters, the Archaeological Museum, the Church of Our Lady of the Castle and the Decorative Arts Collection. Cost: 10€.*

The medieval town is a 'UNESCO World Heritage Monument'. For maps of the attractions in Rhodes Old Town (*see pages 196/7*).

Palace of the Grand Master (*Kastello*)

The Palace, originally a Byzantine fortress, was built at the end of the 7th century below the ancient acropolis. When the Knights of the Order of St. John arrived on the island in the 14th century, they converted the fortress into both the residence for the Grand Master and an administrative headquarters for the knights' order.

In 1856, the palace was destroyed when a large store of gunpowder, kept under the Church of St. John, which was situated opposite, exploded. The building lay in ruins until the late 1930's, when the then Italian administration, rebuilt the palace to its original state, to serve as the residence for the island's Governor.

The rooms on the ground floor house two large permanent exhibitions with the theme "The City of Rodos", the first from its founding in 408 B.C. until the Roman Empire and the second from the 4th century A.D. until the Ottoman occupation in 1522.

During the summer months, as part of the island's summer festivals, the palace is the venue for concerts that range from classical through to contemporary. Details of events will be posted on the 'Rhodes News' page of our website.

Opening Hours: April-October: 08:00-20;00.
Mondays: 09:00-16.00 (*summer season*)
November to April: 08:30-15:00 (*Closed Mondays*)
Admission charge 6€, under 18 free.

Street of the Knights

The Street of the Knights (*Odos Ippoton*) is one of the best preserved medieval streets in Europe. The street is 200 metres in length and runs from the Palace of the Grand Master down to Museum Square. On either side of the street were the medieval inns that housed the knights' "tongues" (*national groups*) that made up the Order of the Knights of St John. These included England, Italy, France, Germany, Auvergne, Aragon, Provence and Castile. At the bottom of the Street in Museum square is the building that housed the 'Hospital of the Knights', which is now the location for the Archaeological Museum of Rhodes.

The street was the centre of political and religious life in the time of the knights, linking as it does the palace with the Church of Our Lady of the Castle. Along its length were the most important public and private buildings within the medieval town. Above the main door to the various inns that line both sides of the street, you will see the shield bearing the crest of the particular nationality of knights that resided in that building.

Archaeological Museum

The Archaeological Museum of Rhodes is housed in the medieval building that served as the Hospital of the Knights of St. John. Building began in 1440 commissioned by Grand Master de Lastic with money bequeathed by his predecessor, Grand Master Fluvian, and was completed in 1489 by Grand Master d'Aubusson.

The building consists of a large central atrium, flanked by arched galleries which today house some of the ancient sculptures and funerary pieces found throughout Rhodes. Toilets for visitors are also situated on the ground floor. Stairways then lead up to the first floor, which consists of one large room, the Infirmary (which would have had up to 100 beds) and twenty small rooms, most with fireplaces that served as the individual bedrooms for the more important patients and administrative rooms.

Today the small rooms house exhibitions of finds dating from all periods of the island's history, discovered during archaeological excavations.

In the museum's garden the visitor will find further sculptures and funerary steles and mosaic floors of the Hellenistic period discovered in Rhodes Town.

Opening times: Summer: 08:00-20:00
Monday: 09:00-16:00
Winter: 08:30-15:00 (*Closed Monday*)
Admission charge: 8€, children under 18 free.

Dome

The Dome (large bandstand), located in Mandraki, hosts a number of music and dance events during the summer months. (please check our website for the latest details)

Moat

The moat and fortifications we see today enclosing Rhodes Old

Town, reached their present complexity in the 16th century. Although it extends down to the sea on both sides, the entire surface area is above sea-level and was consequently never flooded. The circumference of the moat is 2,300 metres (*2,500 yards*) and 70 metres (*77 yards*) at its widest point. This is a walk not to be missed, as it gives the visitor the best view of the formidable fortifications and confirms why this bastion was never breached.

There are three entry and exit points around the circuit, the first is near the taxi rank behind Mandaki harbour, the second is via the Gate Acandia (*Gate Karetou*) and the third is the Kanonia Gate, near the entrance to the Grand Palace.

Entrance to the moat is free and is open all year round.

The **Melina Mercouri theatre**, which is the venue during the summer months for concerts, theatrical shows and dance performances, is situated within the moat (*see page 53*).

City Walls Walk

An alternative or additional walk that offers a superb view of the fortifications and Old Town is along the wall's battlements. The entrance is at the Kanonia Gate and ends at St. John's Gate (*Gate of Agios Ioannou*). The walk is around 1,100 metres. Please ask at the Grand Palace, or one of the Tourist Information offices for the latest information. Admission 2€. Walks between 12:00-15:00.

Rodini Park

Rodini Park is one of the most ancient untouched parts of Rhodes Town and was probably one the first landscaped gardens in the world. The park was the site of the famous Rhodian School of Rhetoric. Here many renowned Greeks and Romans studied. It is recorded that these included Julius Caesar, Cicero, Pompey, Brutus and Cassius (*the two main assassins of Julius Caesar*) and Mark Antony.

The park is a cool and tranquil retreat in the hottest part of the day. Comprising of oleander bushes, cypress, maple, pine trees, water lily covered ponds with ducks and free roaming wild peacocks and a fallow deer enclosure. Sadly though in the last few years, it has not received the care and attention it richly deserves.

The most famous attraction within the park is situated within the necropolis area (*past the football field*). This is a monumental rock-cut tomb from the Hellenistic period, called the Tomb of the Ptolomies.

Admission to the park is free. There is a café on site. (*Closed on Mondays*). The park is located on Lindos Avenue, 3 km from the centre of Rhodes Town. You can take a bus from the harbour front, the cost is 4€.

Acropolis (*see map on page 198*)

The ancient acropolis of Rhodes Town is situated on the western edge of town on the hill known as Monte Smith. The initial archaeology on the site was undertaken by the Italians during their occupation of the island in the early 20th century. Today all archaeological work is administered by the Greek Archaeological Service. There are still large parts of the acropolis site that remain unexcavated and undocumented.

What is known is that at the height of the Hellenistic period, the acropolis consisted of sanctuaries, temples, public buildings, cultivated gardens and spacious public meeting areas and was renowned at the time for its beauty and elegance. In the words of Aelius Aristides, a famous 2nd century A.D. Greek orator, "It was full of fields and groves".

The acropolis today is well known for both the archaeological ruins and a vantage point to view magnificent sunsets.

The most important monuments visible today on the acropolis are listed on the following three pages.

Temple of Athena Polias and Zeus Polieus

The temple stands at the northern most part of the acropolis and was of Doric design and had an east west orientation. The temple originally had colonnades on all four sides and was one of the city's most important shrines, not only serving as a 'house of the gods', but also as a treasury for the city. In 163 B.C. a colossal statue called The Populus Romanus ("The People of Rome") was erected next to the temple. It was 14 metres tall (46 feet) and celebrated both Rome's victory over Macedonia and Rhodes importance within the new Roman world. The temple stood within a larger walled precinct with a stoa (covered walkway or portico) on the east side.

Zeus was the king on the gods and Athena was seen as one of the principle goddesses within Greek mythology. Both were bestowed with many roles and powers, but as Athena Polias and Zeus Polieus, they were also seen as patron gods of the city.

Stoa

Today only the foundation wall of the stoa is preserved, but in ancient times the stoa combined with the monumental temple behind, must have made the whole complex a wondrous site from the city below.

Nymphaea

The Nymphaea consists of four cave-like structures cut into the natural rock. There are communicating passages, a large opening in the central part of the roof and recesses in the interior walls for statues. The grotto was linked to the city's subterranean water-system and contained water cisterns and lush vegetation, which were all seen as important features within the cult and worship of the nymphs.

In Greek mythology nymphs were seen as different from goddesses and were generally regarded as divine spirits who animated nature and could be mischievous. They were associated with groves, water and the underworld.

Temple of Pythian Apollo

On the southwest plateau of Mont Smith, stands the Temple of Pythian Apollo. Part of the northeast section, comprising four columns and parts of the lintel and architrave, have been restored. It was of a similar design to the Temple of Athena Polias and Zeus Polieus, but smaller. In front of the temple is a large rectangular terrace, which was most likely part of the sanctuary enclosure.

In classical Greece Apollo was known as the god of light and of music, but for most Greeks he had a prime function of deterring evil.

Artemision

Below and to the north of the terrace is an area which contained a number of religious buildings including the Artemision, the temple to the goddess Artemis.

Artemis was one of the most widely venerated of the ancient Greek gods. In the classical period Artemis was often described as the daughter of Zeus and Leto, and the twin sister of Apollo. As she was the goddess of the hunt and wild animals, she was often depicted as a huntress carrying a bow and arrows. However, she was also known as the goddess of childbirth, virginity, the protector of young girls and the healer of women.

Odeum (*Odeon*)

Below and to the east of the Temple to Athena is a restored marble Odeum (*small theatre*). It held seating for an audience of around 800. We know from contemporary accounts from elsewhere in Greece that Odeums were venues for small events such as musical and poetry recitals, political discussions and lectures in such subjects as philosophy and rhetoric.

The remains of a much larger theatre are thought to be situated somewhere on the acropolis, within the yet unexcavated sections of the site.

Stadium

The Stadium is situated in front and to the right of the Odeum. It was built in the 3rd century B.C. and was where the city's athletic events were held. The major festival on Rhodes was in honour of the prime patron of the island, the sun god Helios and during his festival the principal athletic event called the 'Alioi Games' was held in the stadium.

The name stadium comes from the Greek measure, the stadion which was 183 metres (*600 feet*) and this stadium is one stadion in length. The original parts of the ancient stadium visible today are the starting mechanism for the athletes, the sphendone *(the rounded end of the stadium where the athletes turned)*, the proedries (*seating for officials*) and some of the lower seats in the auditorium.

The stadium is still used for occasional performances of classical tragedies and other events.

Gymnasium

To the east of the Stadium are the remains of the Gymnasium. Although the west portion of the building was uncovered by the Italians, recent excavations under what had been the site of the modern visitor café, unearthed the northeast section. We now know that it was a large rectangular building measuring around 200 metres square.

Gymnasia in ancient Greece were not only where athletes trained, but were also places for socializing and engaging in intellectual pursuits. The name comes from the ancient Greek term 'gymnos' meaning naked, as athletes competed nude, a practice said to encourage aesthetic appreciation of the male body and a tribute to the gods. However, women were not allowed to participate or spectate during training, or at the games.

Cultural Museums

Modern Art Museum

The Modern Greek Art Museum presents extensive painting and engraving collections not to mention numerous sculptures, drawings and documents of historical value. The works of engraving and painting represent Greek art of the 20th century along with its most eminent artists. Some of the works of art are considered to be of great significance and they are chosen in order to narrate the history of art. The central idea of all these collections is to present the history of Greece through the eyes and the soul of Greek artists of the last century.

Symi Square, Rhodes Old Town
Opening hours: Tuesday-Saturday 08:00-14:00, Friday 17:00-20:00
Closed Sundays and Mondays
Admission charge: 3€

Museum of Decorative Arts, Rhodes

The collection includes furniture and household utensils, woodcarvings, ceramics (*including the renowned Lindos collection*), traditional costumes and embroideries from all over the Dodecanese. The artefacts cover the period from the 17th to the 20th century.

Argyrokastrou Square, Rhodes Old Town. Tel.: 22410 25500
Opening hours, June to end of October, Tues.-Sunday: 09:00-16:00
November to end of May, Tuesday-Sunday: 08:30-15:00
Admission charge: 2€

Other historic & religious buildings in Rhodes Old Town

Church of Our Lady of the Castle

At the bottom of the 'Street of the Knights' is Museum Square where you will find the 'Church of Our Lady of the Castle'. The church was built by the Byzantines in the 11th century. Although mostly of Byzantine architectural design, there are some Gothic elements added at a later date. When the Knights took the island, they established the church as the city's new Catholic Cathedral, renovating and adding amongst other details, a bell tower. Contained within are many fascinating frescoes, added during the centuries by those who have dominated the island.

In the 14th century, a monastery was opened next to the church.

Byzantine Museum

Within the 'Church Our Lady of the Castle' is the Byzantine Museum housing an exhibition of Byzantine and post-Byzantine painting, including icons from the collection of Byzantine antiquities and wall-paintings detached from the churches of the Archangel Michael at Tharri and Ayios Zacharias at Chalki. Architectural sculptures and members (*column capitals, closure slabs, impost blocks, etc.*) dating from the Early Christian period to that of the Knights have been assembled in the courtyard on the north side of the church.

When the Ottomans seized the island in 1522, the church was converted into the Enterum Mosque. They altered little of the main structure, only converting the bell tower into a minaret. Within the grounds of the church you will find remains of a Doric Temple of Athena Polias. This fascinating site features intricate carvings and should not be missed.

The Church of Our Lady of the Bourg

The ruins of Church of Our Lady of the Bourg are situated on both sides of Pindarou Street (*an extension of Aristotelous*) in the Jewish quarter. The church, completed in 1491, was built by the Knights of St. John to give thanks to "Our Lady" (*Saint Mary*), who they believed had led them to victory over the forces of Mehmed II in 1480. Once the largest Catholic Church on Rhodes, the lofty vaults are all that remain of what was once a magnificent Gothic church after it was hit by a British bomb in World War II.

Church of Our Lady of Victory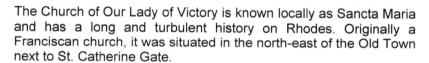

The Church of Our Lady of Victory is known locally as Sancta Maria and has a long and turbulent history on Rhodes. Originally a Franciscan church, it was situated in the north-east of the Old Town next to St. Catherine Gate.

Destroyed after the Ottoman seizure of the island, it wasn't until 1719, when the Franciscan monks were allowed to return to the island, that they requisitioned the site of an ancient church on St. Stephan Hill and in 1743, built the new 'Church of Our Lady of Victory'. The church was enlarged in 1851 and became the principle Catholic Church on Rhodes.

During the earthquake of 1926, the bell tower collapsed and plans were forged to construct a totally new façade. The renovations were completed in 1929 and the Baroque Portal was replaced by a new wrought-iron gate made in Italy.

Evangelismos Church

Evangelismos Church (*also called The Church of the Annunciation*) is located next to the northern breakwater of Mandraki Harbour. It was built in 1925 during the Italian rule. The church is a magnificent example of Gothic architecture. It is similar in design to the church of St. John in Rhodes Old Town and is also dedicated to this saint. The interior was decorated with murals by Fotis Kontoglou, a famous Greek writer, painter and iconographer (*1895-1965*). It is now the main cathedral of Rhodes.

Mosques

There are 13 mosques in Rhodes Old Town. I will cover just two, as well as including nearby Ottoman buildings that are also worthy of a visit (*see maps on pages 196/197*)

Suleymaniye Mosque

The Suleymaniye Mosque is the largest in the town and is situated at the top of Socratous. After the Ottoman conquest of the island in 1522, the Byzantine Church of the Holy Apostles was demolished to make way for the mosque. The mosque's minaret is 34 metres high and is therefore a major landmark in the Old Town.

The mosque was re-built by the Ottomans in 1888, but closed for major restoration work in the 1980's. It re-opened to the public in 2005.

Mustafa Pasha Mosque

Mustafa Pasha Mosque was built in 1765 in Arionos Square, near the Turkish baths in the Old Town. This beautiful mosque was built by Sultan Mustafa III in 1765. The sultan was a devout Muslim, commissioning many mosques during his lifetime.

Fethi Pasha Clock Tower (*Roloi Tower*)

Just around the corner from the Suleymaniye Mosque is the Fethi Pasha Clock Tower (*Roloi Tower*). It was commissioned in 1851 by Fethi Pasha, an Ottoman governor of the island. The tower is open to the public and a superb vantage point for views across the town. Admission charge: 5€, which includes a drink.

Turkish Library

Opposite the mosque on the other side of Socratous is the Turkish Library, built in 1794 and now administered by the Fethi Pasha Foundation. The library houses more than 2,000 Turkish, Arabic and Persian manuscripts and two beautifully illustrated 15/16th century copies of the Koran. The library is open to the public. Admission charge 2€.

Turkish Baths (*Hamam*)

The Baths of Suleiman, also known as the New Baths (*Yenni Hamam*), are the only Turkish Baths on the island. Built in 1558, it is separated into male and female bathing days. Open for men on Monday, Wednesday and Friday and ladies on Tuesday, Thursday and Saturday (*Closed on Sunday*). The baths are heated by an under floor fire. There are masseurs on-hand at an extra charge, but I would suggest you miss this experience!

The cost is around 5€ and you can either bring your own soap and towel, or the baths will supply them on entry (*Closed Sunday*)

Synagogue

Kahal Shalom Synagogue

The Kahal Shalom Synagogue is a Sephardic Jewish synagogue located in the old Jewish Quarter. There has been a Jewish community on Rhodes for more than two millennia and, although they were often persecuted under the Romans and Knights of St. John, they enjoyed peace and prosperity under Ottoman rule. Built in 1577, the Kahal Shalom is Greece's oldest surviving and continuously used synagogue. However, much of the local Jewish community emigrated following the Italian take over the Dodecanese Islands in 1912 and the majority of those who were left were transported by the Germans to Auschwitz during the Second World War.

There is a museum attached to the Synagogue that charts the story of the Jewish community on Rhodes through the centuries.

Museum entrance charge 4€, free for children under 12.

General attractions in Rhodes Town
(in alphabetical order)

Aquarium

The Aquarium of Rodos is located within Rhodes Town at the northern most tip, 1km from Mandraki Harbour. It is one of the most important marine research centres in Greece and draws tens of thousands of visitors each year.

The building is of Art Deco design, by the Italian architect Armando Bernabiti and was constructed between 1934 and 1935, during the Italian occupation of the island.

The visitor section of the Aquarium has been designed in the form of an underwater sea-cave, with rock covered walls encrusted with seashells, creating a feeling for the visitor of being part of a marine environment.

In the underground aquarium the visitor can see many of the species of the marine life of the Aegean Sea.

The Aquarium is administered by the National Centre for Marine Research and is open daily:

The opening hours are:-
1st April until 31st October: 09:00 - 20:30
1st November until 31st March: 09:00 - 16:30

Admission charge: adults: 5.50€. Reduced ticket: 3.50€ (Students/ OAP's). Pre- school children: free

Casino

The Casino of Rodos & Albergo Delle Rose Boutique Hotel are, located on the northern tip of the island just outside Rhodes Town.

The building which used to house the historic Hotel of the Roses has been sumptuously restored. The lower floor is taken up with over 300 slot machines and amusements, whereas the upper floor has 34 gaming tables which include Blackjack, Roulette, Stud Poker and Punto Banco.

A valid identification document such as a passport is required for registering for the gaming tables, with a minimum age of 21.
The slot machine floor is open 24/7.
The upper floor live gaming is open:-
Monday to Friday - 17:00 - 03:00
Saturday - 14:00 - 04:00
Sunday - 12:00 - 03:00
There is an admission charge of 6€ (*local gaming tax*)

Melina Mercouri Theatre and Diagora Stadium

In the Melina Mercouri Theatre, situated in the castle's medieval dry moat and at the Diagora Stadium in Rhodes New Town, cultural events, theatre shows and concerts are held through the summer season. The details are only available during the season and near to the event, so please ask for details at the Tourist Information Offices.

Municipal Cultural Organisation of Rhodes, Tel.: 22410 27427

Old Town Aquarium

As the name implies, this aquarium is in the Old Town, on Agiou Fanourio. Privately run, there are aquaria containing 150 Mediterranean and tropical species, including sharks, stingrays and octopi.

Admission charge: Adults 5€, children 3€, under 5's free

Orca (*Glass bottom boat*)

The Orca is a futuristic looking boat that has a glass viewing port in the bottom of the boat. It is based in Mandraki Harbour, Rhodes

Town, opposite the Post Office. The tours last 30 mins. and leaves every hour visiting some of the most beautiful underwater sightseeing areas around Rhodes island, such as Mandraki Harbour, Elli beach, the Port of Rhodes and the Lighthouse of Rhodes. The boat has a toilet on board.

Trips run from 10:30-18:00
Cost: adults 10€, children 5€
Tel.: (*0030*) 6944146148

Insider tip: In high season it is advisable to book as the boat's capacity is only 25.

Sound and Light Show (*Son et Lumière*)

Sound and Light is a popular multi-media show presenting the history of the Knights of the Order of St. John. The theatre is just outside and below the walls of the Old Town, in the gardens of the Palace of the Grand Masters, near Alexandrous Square (*map on page 196*).

The show is presented in the evenings, Monday to Saturday, from April to October. The show is narrated in a number of languages including English, Greek, French, German, Italian and Swedish at different times of the evening. The times are not fixed, but the two English shows per evening are usually at around 21:15 and 23:15. The shows last around 50 minutes. Tel.: 22410 21922

Traditional Folk Dance Theatre

The internationally acclaimed Traditional Folk Dance Theatre of Rhodes is situated in Rhodes Old Town, just behind the Turkish baths. The theatre presents performances in traditional dress of authentic Greek dancing, song and live music.

The theatre is open from May to early October
Tel.: 22410 20157
Admission charge and times depend on the performance.

Archaeological sites around the island
(in alphabetical order)

Ancient Kamiros (*see map on page 200*)

Kamiros, with Ialysos and Lindos, were the three great ancient cities of Rhodes. The ruins of the city and neighbouring necropolis were excavated in 1859 in what had become a heavily wooded area, which had protected the underlying archaeology over the centuries. Homer, in his epic 'The Iliad', described the city as "arginoeis", a reference to the fertility of the surrounding area. Kamiros was the birthplace of many famous Greeks, including the great poets Peisandros and Anaxandrides.

Although Mycenaean tombs and artefacts have been found in the general area, there was certainly a permanent settlement on the site from at least the early Archaic period. However, the city only reached its zenith during the 6th and 5th centuries B.C. The ruins we see today are mainly from the Hellenistic period, as an earthquake in 226 B.C. devastated the city, leading to its extensive rebuilding.

The new city followed the rules of Hellenistic urban design, introduced by the architect and urban planner Hippodamus (*498 - 408 B.C.*). The 'Hippodamium' design brought order to urban planning, dividing the total area into districts, with these sub-divided up into a chequer-board of regular spaced parallel streets.

Kamiros was divided into three main districts, the lower level with religious and public buildings and spaces such as the agora, the slopes of the surrounding hills, which were designated for residential and private buildings and the acropolis, as was traditional, reserved for religious buildings. The city's preserved sewer system and a large water cistern, testify to the quality and sophistication of planning which went into the new city.

On the north-west of the agora called "The Fountain Square", the 6 columns visible today were part of a Doric temple of the 3rd or 2nd century B.C., dedicated to Apollo.

During excavations, the remains of the sanctuary of the goddess Athena Kamirada were found on the summit of the acropolis.

When the three cities of Kamiros, Ilyasos and Lindos merged in 408 B.C. into one more powerful city-state, Kamiros started to decline, although it remained inhabited until the reign of the Byzantine Emperor Justinian.

Opening times: Tuesday to Sunday, 08:00-19:40
Mondays 08:00-14:40
Admission charge: 6€, children 3€.

Filerimos (*see pages 72 and 199*)

One of the most important and picturesque archaeological sites on the island is only 1km south of the centre of the modern town of Ialysos (*also known as Trianda*), on the hill of **Filerimos**.

Ancient Ialysos was one of the three ruling cities of Rhodes, the birthplace of many famous historical Greeks including Diagoras, the greatest Olympic champion of antiquity as well as of Timokreon, a celebrated poet. The city was founded around the 15th century B.C by the Mycenaeans (*see page 7*). Situated on a 267 metre high hill, Filerimos is heavily wooded with many species of trees including cypress and pine and a population of wild peacocks. As you walk up the hill you will find the remains of a **Temple to Zeus Polieus and Athena Polias**, the remnants of Byzantine fortifications, the 14th century **Monastery of Filerimos**, built by the Knights of St. John, and a path of cypress trees that chart the first 12 stages of the 'Passion of Christ'. Steps then lead up to the highest point, a terrace containing a monumental 70m high cross of stone. The cross has an internal staircase which leads up to a viewing area near the top. From here there are wonderful panoramic views of Rhodes. On a clear day you can even see Lindos, 35km to the south.

The Church of Our Lady at Filerimos has four chapels, the outer of which was built by Grand Master d'Aubusson in the 14th century. The innermost still has the earlier Christian church's fish design mosaic floor, the fish being one of the earliest symbols of Christianity. At the rear of the church are the cloisters and the monks' cells. In front of the church is a sunken 6th century A.D. cruciform baptismal font.

This monastery was destroyed during the Ottoman occupation, but later rebuilt by the Italians who invited Capuchin monks (*an order of Franciscans*) to administer the monastery.

The remains in front of the church are those of the Temple of Zeus Polieus and Athena Polias. All three ancient cities of Rhodes had a temple to these principle gods. This temple was larger than those at both Lindos and Kamiros, but smaller than that built later on the acropolis of the new merged island capital, above modern day Rhodes Town. The temple had a tetrastyle entrance (*four columns*) in front of the pronaos (*porch*), with a further four columns that formed the entrance to the cella (*central temple area*). The cella contained the principle cult statues of the two gods. The remains of a paved floor from an even earlier Phoenician temple can be seen in front of one of the rectangular statue bases.

In front of the temple to Athena Polias and Zeus Polieus is the small underground Byzantine chapel of Agios Georgios, whose walls are decorated with 14th century frescoes by the Knights of St. John.

Opening times: 08:00-19:00.
Admission charge: 6€, children 3€.

Insider tip: The resident monks make a very tasty cocktail, which you are welcome to try.

Lindos (*see map on page 201*)

A visit to Lindos and especially a walk up to the acropolis is highly recommended. You can easily spend the rest of the day exploring all the scenic alleyways that weave their way through the village.

The acropolis of Lindos stands imposingly on a 116 metre high rock outcrop overlooking the village below. Its history extends back to the Neolithic age, although the few finds from this period testify to its unimportance at this time.

It wasn't until the Mycenaean occupation of the island (*15th century B.C.*) that Lindos seems to have become an important settlement. Legend has it that this was when the Sanctuary to Athena was founded. However, it wasn't until the arrival of the Dorians in the 10th century that the settlement flourished. By the 8th century it was a major trading centre with contacts across the Eastern Mediterranean. The Archaic period (*800-480 B.C.*) was the 'Golden Age' for Lindos, with the city-state establishing colonies across the Mediterranean, one of the principal being at Gela in Sicily.

In the 6th century the city-state was ruled by a man called Kleovoulos, who become known as one of the "Seven Sages of the Ancient World", a title given by ancient Greeks to seven early 6th century philosophers, statesmen and law-givers who were renowned for their wisdom.

As you climb the path up to the acropolis, you will come to a terrace (*just after the ticket office*). On your right is the unique 2nd century B.C monumental engraving of a Trireme (*the common war-galley of the time*). This confirms the importance to Lindos of its naval power to protect the city-states maritime trade.

In 408 B.C., the three island city-states of Ilyasos, Kameros and Lindos merged into one and a new capital was founded on the site of modern-day Rhodes Town. This saw the beginning of the decline of Lindos as a political and economic power. However, the sanctuary of Athena continued to be the principle religious centre on the island.

By 200 B.C. the acropolis attained the form we see the ruins of today, dominated by the massive temple of Athena Lindia, the Propylaea (*monumental gateway*), the great Hellenistic stoa and a Roman temple (*popularly thought to be dedicated to the Emperor Diocletian*).

The acropolis is surrounded by a monumental fortification wall contemporary with the building of the Propylaea and the stairway which leads to the entrance of the sanctuary. A Roman inscription proclaims that the square towers and wall were repaired at the expense of Aelius Hagetor, the priest of Athena in the 2nd century A.D.

During the rule of the Knights of Saint John, the existing fortifications were strengthened with extra towers and the cyclopean walls were strengthened. It was at this time that the Byzantine Church of St. John was built on the ruins of an earlier 6th century church.

The Ottomans, after capturing the island, adopted the castle and continued to use the port as a major trading centre on the island. Lindos' maritime prosperity continued until well into the 19th century.

As you view the acropolis from the village, to the right and above St. Paul's Bay are the ruins of the ancient amphitheatre. Built in the Hellenistic period with 27 tiers of seating, it had a capacity of around 2,000. The size of the theatre confirms the large population that lived in the city at this time. Near to the amphitheatre are the remains of a temple from the $2/3^{rd}$ century B.C.

Opposite the Acropolis, on Krana Hill, are the ruins of a large tomb thought to have been for a wealthy family of the Hellenistic period.

Insider tip: *Make sure you are wearing good non-slip walking shoes. The path up is cobbled and slippery, as the cobbles have been worn ultra smooth by the thousands of tourists who visit the site. Also, make sure you take water with you, as the climb up is tiring, especially in height of summer.*

You can take a donkey ride up to the acropolis (*although you will come away smelling a little like a stable*). If you decide to walk, the path is steep, but not too hard going if you take a break along the way. Admission charge: 12€, under 18 free.

When you arrive at Lindos by car, you have to park at the top of the hill which leads down to the village. The main island bus service and coaches also drop visitors opposite the main car park. You can either walk down to the village, take the short connecting bus service, or a taxi.

High Season times are: 08:00 - 19:40, Closed Monday from 14:40. Later in the season the site closes earlier.
To check times phone: 22410 75674 or 22410 31048

Insider tip: Lindos is the most visited tourist attraction on the island after Rhodes Town, so if you want to enjoy the village in relative tranquillity, I would advise arriving early (08:00), well before the hoards of tourist coaches descend on the village.

There is a bus and boat service from Rhodes Town to Lindos.

Vroulia

Vroulia is an ancient settlement whose remains are located at the southernmost tip of Rhodes, opposite the island of Prassonisi.

The name of Vroulia is modern, the ancient name is unknown. A wall about 300 metres long encloses a coastal strip of land to the south west. Except for a section at the west end, the wall is perfectly straight, and against its inner face was a continuous row of simple houses, consisting at most of a couple of rooms with a little court in front. At a distance of about 25 metres was a second row of houses running parallel. The main gate was probably at the point where the wall changes direction; and nearby is a walled area containing two altars, and an adjacent enclosure which may be an agora (*market place*). Pottery dates all these structures to not much later than 700 B.C. Vroulia was only a small town, no doubt subordinate to one of the major cities, presumably Lindos.

Today the small harbour below is a safe haven for small fishing boats.

Permanently accessible. Free entrance.

The castles of Rhodes
(*in alphabetical order, map on page 199*)

As Rhodes was heavily fortified by the Knights of St. John, you will find numerous castles and fortified towers dotted around the island's landscape. Most were built on the sites of previous fortifications from the many different factions who have ruled the island. On the following pages I cover those that are in my view worth a visit.

Insider tip: *Take extra care, especially with children, as the battlements on all the castles have no safety features. Also as the castles are built on the top of hills, it is advisable to wear good walking shoes.*

Archangelos Castle

Archangelos Castle is located in Kerami, at an altitude of 200 metres above sea level and a short distance from the coast. It is built on a rocky outcrop 217 meters high, east of the village of Archangelos.

As recorded in the decree of the Knights of St. John, it was built in the 15th century by the grand Master Ntemily, to effectively protect the villagers from attacks by pirates and ultimately the threat from the Ottoman Empire.

Admission is free

Castle of Asklipio

The castle is perched on a hill 250 metres above the village of Asklipio. Like most castles on the island it was built in 15th century by the Grand Master Pierre d'Aubusson in 1479 on the site of an ancient beacon tower. The castle was used by the Knights to protect the residents of the nearby village and as an observation post covering a wide section of coastline and the inland roads.

Admission is free

Castle of Feraklos

Towering above the Bay of Haraki is the Castle of Feraklos. This was one of the best fortified castles of the Knights of St. John. The castle was mainly used by the knights as a prison to hold prisoners-of-war, but also foreign merchants who had transgressed the rules of the knights.

The castle proved its formidable fortifications during Suleiman Magnificent's siege of the island in 1522, holding out for months after the fall of Rhodes Town. Finally though, in 1523, the castle was taken and the knights and their retinue were slaughtered. Prince Murat of Turkey, who had been residing in the castle whilst planning the overthrow of Suleiman, was captured and subsequently hanged, along with the members of his family. The castle was never occupied again and consequently fell into decay.

The climb to the top of the castle is quite strenuous and difficult and therefore I would not recommend it for the faint-hearted, young or elderly. There is only one entrance and to get to it, you have to climb a short but uneven flight of steps. The interior of the castle is full of rubble and is overgrown, but there are some wonderful views from this vantage point.

Admission is free.

Castle of Kritinia (*Kastelos*)

The medieval castle of Kritinia is located on the north western coast, 2 km northwest and 131 metres above the village of Kritinia.

The castle was built by the Knights of Saint John in the 14th century, incorporating both Venetian and Byzantine architectural styles. Built on three separate levels, each was assigned to a different "tongue" of knights (*nationality*). Inside are the remains of the Church of Saint Paul used by the resident knights.

The castle is in ruins, but that's part of the charm and compared to other castles on the island it is easy to get to. A short flight of steep steps from the small car park brings you to the castle, where there are magnificent views of the surrounding countryside and Aegean.

The sunsets are especially beautiful from the castle battlements. There is a small café just down from the car park.

Admission is free at the time of writing, although a ticket booth has recently been added!

In late June the castle hosts a medieval festival. Information will be posted in 'Rhodes News' on our website in June.

Castle of Monolithos

The castle is perched at the top of a 250 metre high rock (*820 feet*), near to the village of Monolithos and is accessed by a path and steps, taking around 10 minutes to reach the castle. It was built by the Knights of the Order of St. John in 1476, on the site of a previous Byzantine castle, to control the sea passage and protect the west coast against pirate raids.

Once again the castle never fell to attackers, though sadly it is time that has taken its toll on this once proud outpost of the knights. Inside the ruins there is little to see, other than a small whitewashed chapel dedicated to Saint Panteleimon and some cisterns that supplied water to the garrison. However, the castle is worth a visit for three reasons, the magnificent views, the enchanting sunsets and the fragrance of pine and herbs that scent the air.

Admission is free.

Insider tip: If you visit for the magnificent sunsets, leave before it gets totally dark and take a torch for safety.

Below the castle you will find a small stone building that houses a café. The nearest restaurants though are in Monolithos village.

Beware of the road that leads from the castle down to the beaches, it snakes down the valley with steep drops and no barriers and is not for those who suffer from vertigo.

Natural island attractions *(alphabetically, map on page199)*

Apolakkia Reservoir

Two kilometres north from the village of Apolakkia is the artificial reservoir of Apolakkia, also known as Ancient Eleousa.

The dam was built by the Italians and completed in 1989 to supply water to the region. Through the years it has evolved into an important wetland, playing host to a large number of migratory birds each year.

The dam is ideal for sailing and other water sports, but is also a beautiful area for walking.

The lake is ecologically important due to its many rare wild flowers and fauna and a rare endangered fish the "ghizani", which only lives in the fresh waters on Rhodes. The lake and surrounding area has been included in the Natura 2000 network as a protected area.

There is a Water Sports Centre on the lake and numerous sporting activities are hosted at the lake every year.

Near the lake is the small Byzantine chapel of 'Saint George Vardas', built in 1290 A.D.

Bee Museum

The people of Rhodes are proud of their beekeeping heritage, so much so that they have created the 'Museum of Natural History of the Bee', the only such museum in Greece.

The exhibits cover the science of beekeeping from the 1800's up to modern times, including demonstrations of old and present apiculture methods, such as the management of beehives, honey extraction, the production of wax, royal jelly, propolis (bee glue) and more.

The museum is located in the village of Pastida, just off the road linking Faliraki with the airport.

Museum opening times:
Monday-Saturday: 08:30-17:00
Sunday: 10:00-15:00 (June-September)
Tel.: +30 22410 48200

Kalithea Springs

Kalithea Springs is located in the bay of Kalithea, just 9km from Rhodes Town. The thermal springs of Kalithea have been known since antiquity for their healing powers. In 1927, Mario Lago, the Italian governor of Rhodes, commissioned the renowned architect Pietro Lombardi to restore the springs to their former glory. The Kalithea Springs once again became popular and remained in operation until 1967, after which it fell into disrepair. For film buffs, the ruins were used as one of the locations in both the "Guns of Navarone" and "Escape to Athena".

In July of 2007, after extensive refurbishment, it once again re-opened to the public as a museum, conference centre and wedding venue. Creating what is now a beautiful 'retreat', rather than a medicinal spa.

The architecture and decoration is very attractive, with pebble stone mosaics, beautiful gardens, a large rotunda hall, terracing, spacious patio area, fountains and a grand entrance stairway. The complex is situated overlooking a beautiful cove and being protected by the headland is a sun-trap, making it an excellent place to sun-bathe or just chill out. The beach has a gentle incline and therefore good for families with young children. Sunbeds and umbrellas are available to hire.

The complex's cove and beaches attract hundreds of visitors daily and is a good spot for snorkelling and there is a diving school. A nicely decorated café/restaurant on the terracing serves meals and snacks and down at the picturesque harbour there is a café where you can sit and relax and take in the wonderful scenery.

Admission charge: 3€. There is a shop onsite that sells souvenirs and beach products.

Insider tip: *The mobile canteen in the car park sells drinks and snacks at lower prices than in the Kalithea Springs complex.*

Farma Animal Park

Farma (formerly Rhodes Ostrich Farm and Park) is located on the road from the west coast to the Valley of the Butterflies and next door to the Valley. The park covers an area of 34,000 sq. metres with ostriches as well as many other animal species such as camel, donkeys, deer, kangaroos, boars, pony, lama, dwarf goats, sheep and hares, many of which can be fed and stroked by guests. There is also the Farm's Herbs Garden to visit, plus an onsite restaurant.

Open daily, 09:00 until sunset. Admission is free for Infants (under 3 years), 4 euro for children (3-12 years) and 7 euro for persons older than 12. *However, on presentation of this book, you will receive a 15% discount.* Website: www.farma-rhodes.gr

Rhodian Miniature Horses

The Rhodian Horse (*Equus caballus*) is one of the smallest horses in the world. Domesticated, their use declined in the last century due to farm mechanisation, leading to them being released and left to fend for themselves in the forests around Archangelos. This has resulted in a dramatic collapse of their population and sadly left the species on the edge of extinction.

This pygmy horse, sometimes as short as 0.8m and rarely attaining a height of 1.15m has been placed under the protection of Faethon, a local association established in 2001 for the purpose of saving this animal of rare charm and elegance. There are fewer than 10 horses left on the island, but a breeding program has already been successful, with the first birth recorded in 2002. Rhodian Horses may be visited at the Equestrian Club of Archangelos (*at Napes*) in a specially designed public viewing area.

Seven Springs

Located 30km southeast of Rhodes Town near to Archangelos, Seven Springs is one of the most charming destinations on Rhodes, offering a magical landscape and a peaceful cool oasis, even in the height of summer. The lake is surrounded by pine forests and lush vegetation, a lovely place for a walk or the opportunity to just chill out. Occasionally the tranquillity is broken by the calls of wild peacocks, or of the geese and ducks that inhabit the lake.

The lake, which is man-made, was constructed by the Italians to supply fresh water to the nearby village of Kolymbia. It is fed all year round via a tunnel from the natural springs higher up. The lake is deep and not recommended as a safe place to swim. Visitors can walk through the aqueduct tunnel to the lake, or take the path over the hill. There is a café serving light refreshments.

Insider tip: A note of warning to anyone who suffers the slightest from claustrophobia. The tunnel is 186 metres long and once in, it is pitch-dark and difficult, if not impossible, to turn round to exit the same way!

Toy Museum

In late 2016, the Rhodes Toy Museum opened in the village of Archipoli. The museum contains over 5,000 Greek toys from the 1930's up to the 1990's, a games room with antique slot-machines and a range of interactive games for children. The museum also holds a number of events for children during the summer season.

The village of Archipoli lies on the road that runs from the Valley of the Butterflies to Seven Springs. Tel.: (0030) 698 570 2210.

Valley of the Butterflies (*Petaloudes*)

The Valley of the Butterflies lies 5km southeast of the village of Theologus and 25km from Rhodes Town. The valley is the beautiful habitat of what is actually a moth, Panaxia Quadripunctaria, a subspecies of the Jersey Tiger Moth. The main difference between these very similar species is that butterflies are active in the daytime, whereas moths are generally nocturnal. Of course the Valley of the Butterflies also sounds much more attractive than the Valley of the Moths!

This species of moth makes its appearance from mid-June to mid-September in the daytime to mate and lay eggs. August though is the principal month during which thousands of the beautiful moths emerge from their cocoons and put on their magnificent display of colour and delicate flight.

The nature reserve consists of specially designed trails and wooden bridges, ponds filled with water lilies, waterfalls with crystal clear waters and rich vegetation of unequalled beauty. During springtime, the caterpillar stage of the moth feed on the local vegetation of arbutus, myrtle and rush. As the dry summer season unfolds at the end of May, the fully formed moths start to make their appearance in the form recognizable to us.

Sadly, over the last few years the population has been constantly in decline due to several factors, one of the most important being the disturbance by visitors to the reserve. This is forcing the butterflies to fly all day, consuming valuable energy that they require for reproduction and therefore affecting the long-term sustainability of the population. To try to reach a balance, whereby visitors are allowed access to enjoy the amazing spectacle, but the moths remain undisturbed strict rules are enforced prohibiting visitors from engaging in any acts such as shouting, clapping, or whistling.

The Museum of Natural History of the island of Rhodes is located at the entrance of the nature reserve. Here visitors have the opportunity to appreciate the life-cycle of this wonderful insect and the whole eco-system of the area in which it lives.

Opening Hours: 08:00-16:00 (*May until 31st of October*)
Admission charge before the moths appear: 3€
Admission charge after mid-June: 5€. Telephone: 22410 82822

Villages around the island *(in alphabetical order)*

Whilst there are a total of 44 villages on the island, on the following pages I have chosen 14 that are worth a visit. (*see map on page 2*). However, to help further, below I have ranked the top five villages which have the most to offer visitors.

1. **Lindos**
2. **Kalithea**
3. **Archangelos**
4. **Embonas**
5. **Lardos**

Insider tip: The taking of photographs inside Orthodox churches is forbidden.

Afandou

Afandou is the second largest municipality after Rhodes Town and Ialysos, with a community of around 6,500. An attractive village surrounded by groves of fruit and olive trees, it was founded during the period when Rhodes suffered from pirate raids and was therefore sited out of view from the sea. Afandou translates as "invisible".

Afandou was once known as a centre for carpet making, but now the locals rely on tourism, hence the village has many tavernas, bars, tourist shops and a 'folklore' museum.

There are two churches in the area that are worth visiting, both are called the **'Church of Our Lady'**. The first an Orthodox church situated in Afandou's attractive village Square. The second is a **catholic church** situated on the road that leads to the beach. The latter was built on the site of an early Christian basilica and houses a number of 17th century murals on its walls. It also plays host to a large flock of birds that permanently nest there.

For those who enjoy walking, take a stroll up the hill from the village to Profitis Ilias. From the top there are beautiful views of the surrounding countryside and coast.

At the end of June, the village of Afandou is the location of the annual festival in celebration of the locally produced apricot. The **'Apricot Festival'** is held in the afternoon in the idyllic setting of the Monastery of Our Lady Catholic, located near the beach of Afandou. Please check our website nearer to the end of June for confirmation of the details of the festival.

Apolakkia

Apolakkia is a small village of around 300 inhabitants situated near Lindos and built in a natural bowl, from which it gets its name. Its main claim to fame is the nearby dam behind which has formed a **picturesque lake** called the Apolakkia Reservoir (*see page 64*) and a habitat for a rich diversity of bird and animal life, unique to this part of the island. The lake is 1750m long and 200m wide and is located 3km northeast from the village. The whole area has been designated a nature reserve, making it a haven for bird watchers, or just those seeking the perfect setting for a swim and a relaxing break from sight-seeing. Next to the lake is the 13th century Byzantine church of **Agios Georgios**.

Most of the village houses are of a traditional design, but in the square is **The Old Italian House**, built by the Italians when they controlled the island and one of the most attractive buildings in Apolakkia. The old windmills and monasteries that dot the village make this a wonderful setting for a leisurely stroll.

The village plays host to the annual **'Watermelon Festival'** in mid July at the local lake. During the festival there will be live music, song and dance, watermelon sculpture competitions and of course amongst other attractions sweet watermelon to enjoy. Details will be posted on our website prior to the event.

Archangelos

Archangelos is located on the east coast, 30 km south of Rhodes Town. Its population is 5,500 making it the fourth largest town after the capital Rhodes, Ialysos and Afandou. The town is named after its patron saint, the Archangel Michael, whose church with its beautiful tiered belfry, is the most prominent building in the town. This design of church tower is traditional on Rhodes, as on other islands in the Dodecanese group, but this is certainly one of the prettiest. Cross vaulting, instead of the more usual barrel vaulting, is very much a feature of architecture on the island.

Initial impressions as you enter the town may not initially impress, but my advice is to "dig a little deeper" and explore the side alleys, narrow streets and picturesque squares of the town and you will find a very different world, one where the locals still follow a very traditional way of life.

Four further attractions in or near the town are, the **Real Olive Press** factory, which is open free to the public during the summer months as an olive oil museum and shop (on Georgiou Papandreou Street), the **Cave of Koumellos**, the **Church of Saint John**, which has some beautiful 14th century frescoes and lastly, on a hill above the town, and roughly a 15 minute walk from the centre, the **Castle of St. John**, built in the 15th century by the Knights Hospitallers.

Tsambika Monastery is perched 270m high, on the summit of a hill just off the road from Archangelos to Kolymbia. Take the road from Archangelos to Kolymbia and after 4km there is a turning to the right that takes you up to the monastery (*1.2km*). A short walk then takes you up to a tiny white Byzantine church on the summit. From this vantage point there are spectacular views of the coast, both north to Kolymbia and south to distant Lindos. The church contains an 11th century icon of the Virgin Mary. Tradition has it that it was found on the mountain by a couple who could not have children, but after finding the icon the wife bore a child. It is now believed that if a childless woman walks barefoot up the mountain to pray to the Virgin, she will then be blessed with children. This tradition is so strong that many children in the area are named after the monastery, Tsambikos for a boy and Tsambika for a girl, a name unique to Rhodes.

The Virgin's Saint Day is the 7th September, when a festival is held.

Asklipio

Asklipio is situated 64km southeast of Rhodes Town and inland from Kiotari. The village is named after the Greek god of medicine and healing, Asklepios. It is believed from artefacts discovered in the area that there was a temple or sanctuary (*as on Kos*) to the god in the area, but as yet no remains have been found.

Today, the village is better known for the remains of a **medieval castle** built by the Knights Hospitallers in the 13th century. The castle dominates the hill above the village from where there are panoramic views of the eastern coastal area. Now though it is goats that walk the battlements, not knights.

Next to the large village square is the **Byzantine Church of the Dormition**, built in 1060 and recently restored. It contains some magnificent examples of orthodox frescoes. Next door to the church is the old village olive press and a small **folklore museum**.The main festival days in the village are the transfiguration of Christ on the 5/6th August and the Assumption of the Virgin Mary on the 15th August.

Dimylia

Located in a valley next to Kokkinisti Springs is the village of Dimylia. The village is built on the east side of the Prophet Elias mountain. It is a traditional and picturesque village with many Greek tavernas and traditional houses. Crooked little alleyways, paved with quarry stone, are always neat and tidy. The profusion of flowers that decorate the village, make the views even more impressive. In the spring and summer, these pervade the air with their strong fragrances.

Dimylia probably took its name from a temple dedicated to an ancient god. Remains of the temple were found in the courtyard of the **Laografiko Museum** in Dimylia. In the same area, there are also the remains of a **byzantine castle**.

In late September the village hosts the annual 'Feast of the Nut' festival, which celebrates the locally grown walnuts.

Embonas

Embonas is the highest village on the island at around 450 metres and is situated in the foothills of Mount Attavyros. It is a picturesque village and one of the best to view the traditional architecture of Rhodes. In the main untouched by tourism, the village's daily routine continues unaltered, with some locals still dressing in the **traditional costumes** of the island.

On the way to the village you will pass by many vineyards as is lies at the heart of the wine producing area and is renowned for producing some of the finest wines and raisins on Rhodes.

Embonas has excellent conditions for grape cultivation and during harvest time the village streets are filled with baskets of grapes, as they wait to be spread out in the yards to dry in the sun.

One of the largest wineries in the region is Emery, which offer guided tours and the chance to purchase a bottle or two to take home (*if it makes it that far*). Three smaller **traditional wineries** in the village are, Alexandris, Kounakis and Merkouris. If you are not driving, you can also add to the experience by tasting the local strong spirit called Suma, which is made from the pomace (*leftovers*) from the wine making process.

The village is also famous for its manufacture of embroidery and hand-woven rugs, many examples of which you will see as you explore the village. The village also has a **folklore museum**.

During the middle of September each year there is a wine festival held in Embonas. You can be entertained by performances of the celebrated local dance groups as well as join in with the feasting and of course 'sampling' the produce of the grapes.

Ialysos (*Ialissos*) (*see also page 56*)

Ialysos (*also known as Trianda*) is the second largest town on the island after Rhodes Town. Located on the north-western coast around 5km from the capital, Ilyasos is dominated by the large hotel complexes that line this part of the coast. The town has become, in all but name, a suburb of Rhodes Town.

Ialysos was one of the first three ancient cities to be founded in around the 15th century B.C by the Mycenaeans (*see page 7*). **Filerimos**, one of the most important and picturesque archaeological sites on the island and only 1km south of the centre of the modern town. Situated on a 267 metre high hill, Filerimos is heavily wooded with many species of trees including cypress pine and olive and plays host to a population of wild peacocks. Even if archaeology is not your 'thing', Filerimos is a beautiful setting for a walk.

Kalithia

The village of Kalithia is defined by narrow alleys and numerous monuments. A charming village, with most of its cafés, bars and tavernas located around the village square.

The oldest written mention to this area comes from the year 1474 when the village is referred to as Calathies, or Calaties. The name in Greek means deserted castle and on the imposing acropolises of Sarantapihos and Erimokastro, there are the very high outer walls of the **castle**, built by the Crusaders to protect the village against attack.

One local church dates back to the 16th century, namely the Church of the Metamorphosis of the Saviour, which has some beautifully preserved icons from that period.

The Patron Saint of Kalithia is Stavros (*translated* as *"the cross"*) and on the 13th September the village holds the Festival of the Honourable Cross.

On the west of the village is the **Eleousa Monastery**. Two 'coats of arms' from the time of the Knights guard the entrance, whilst inside are some unique murals. You should also not neglect visiting the stalactite cave of St. George, which is the oldest known Neolithic dwelling on the island, dating back to 3,500 B.C.

Laerma

Laerma is a small traditional village 10km from Lardos and around 15km from Lindos. Built on a hill surrounded by beautiful pine forests, its main 'claim to fame' is the nearby **Monastery of Thari**.

Thari is the largest monastery on the island and is situated in one of the most beautiful areas of the island, 4km southwest of Laerma. It was built in the 13th century, on the ruins of much older religious buildings from at least the 9th century. The north and south walls are the oldest within the present building, being from the 12th century. The dome, the apse and the nave are decorated with exquisite frescoes and some areas of the church have as many as four layers of artistic work, the earliest from 1100.

There are a number of legends regarding the founding of the monastery. One recounts that a Byzantine Princess, whilst visiting the area, was cured of a terminal illness. After what was seen as a miracle, she happened to drop her ring and in veneration of her cure, the monastery was founded on the spot where it landed.

Centuries after construction, it is now expanding with the addition of accommodation. It is a tranquil place to stop and there are picnic facilities available. Free entry. Open from 08:00 to sunset

Lardos

Lardos is situated inland, 10km west of Lindos. It offers all the facilities you would expect of a modern holiday resort. There are tavernas, cafés, tourist shops, pharmacies, exchange facilities and car, motorbike, and bicycle hire companies.

Village life is centred around the wide tree lined village square where many of the locals still go to draw natural spring water from the fountain; preferring it to the perfectly drinkable piped water supply. You will find many of the friendly locals enjoy sitting in the cafeneions in the square, drinking Greek coffee, or the local ouzo, while talking and playing Tavli (*the equivalent of backgammon*).

Local bands are known to spontaneously turn up in the evening and play live music in the square. The local hotels also offer evening entertainment such as discos and Karaoke evenings. Lindos, with its more extensive night-life, can easily be easily reached by taxi or bus.

The village also has a **Folklore Museum,** on the road to Pefkos, opposite the mini-golf. The brainchild and labour of love of one local resident, a guy named Panagiotis, who is passionate about his village's heritage and history.

Lindos

This traditional village, with its whitewashed houses, the captain's houses with their pebble mosaic courtyards, its Byzantine churches and cobblestone streets, lies at the foot of the ancient acropolis (*see map on page 201*).

Although most tourists visit Lindos for the ancient acropolis (*page 57*), the village is a wonder to explore, set as it is in such a dramatic natural landscape and enhanced by the picturesque architecture and myriad of colourful alleyways. You will find the most important historical monuments on the acropolis, but interesting buildings are scattered at various points throughout the town.

In the heart of the village is the domed **Church of Our Lady (Panagia)**, just off the main square. This fourteenth-century church has a dark interior with a black and white pebbled floor and is decorated with 18th century frescoes by Gregori of Symi, depicting over 80 scenes from the bible.

Papakonstandis Mansion, one of Lindos' famous Captains' houses dates from 1626 and has been turned into a museum to present the culture and traditional house design of the village. It has a beautiful interior with painted wooden ceilings and Arabesque designs.

Sadly, Lindos' fame has meant that throughout the summer months, hordes of tourists descend on the village every day. With them has come a plethora of shops selling cheap souvenirs and higher prices charged in the tavernas and bars. That aside, you can't say you have truly seen Rhodes without visiting Lindos. Therefore my advice would be to arrive early, before the coach tours, when you will be able to admire its beauty in a more tranquil atmosphere.

The village is famous for its ceramic plates, which have historically been more for decoration than for the table. Traditionally the main room (*the Sala*) of the village houses have their walls decorated with the family's finest plates. Modern reproductions can be bought in the local souvenir shops.

Insider tip: Wear good walking shoes as the streets are cobbled and they can play havoc with the soles of your feet.

Lindos comes alive at night with many chill-out bars, music bars and nightclubs. There are **three nightclubs**, Amphitheatre, which is just outside the village, Glow Club and Arches. The latter two are in the village and sound-proofed, as local laws prohibit noise after midnight.

In mid-June, the village hosts its annual 'Lindos Music Week', which features a wide range of contemporary tribute bands. Concerts take place at a designated bar or hotel in Lindos. There is also a 'Greek Night' with a BBQ and a music quiz to keep you entertained. Details will be posted on our website prior to the event.

Monolithos

Monolithos is situated 73km from Rhodes Town and 3km from the beach at Fourni. Built in a natural amphitheatre in the surrounding hills, the village is small, but attractive with stone built houses with whitewashed courtyards, resplendent in summer with geraniums and bougainvillea. There are a few tavernas in the village.

However, the main tourist attraction is the **mediaeval castle of Monolithos**, which translates as "lonely rock" (*see page 63*). The castle is built on a 250 metre high outcrop of rock in front of the village and has a small cark park at the bottom of rock.

Fournis is a quiet beach just below Monolithos consisting of pebbles, but beware, the road that leads down to the beach is a little treacherous and not for the faint hearted.

Salakos

Salakos is a small village with a population of around 350 and lies at the foot of Prophitis Ilias (*the mountain of the prophet Elijah*) 40km south west of Rhodes Town. Surrounded by olive groves and vineyards, Salakos is famous for its fine walnuts and in the past, its hand-made furniture. The heart of this pretty village is its shady square, with fig trees and an unusual tri-bowl spring-water fount. Time seems to have stood still here as you still see grandmothers in headscarves grinding wheat, or baking in the traditional wood-fired ovens.

You will find Salakos a charming place to visit, natural springs, lush vegetation, olive groves and vineyards, all add to the idyllic landscape. There are some beautiful walks around the village including visiting the natural spring called "Nymph".

Close to the edge of the village is the **Cave of Makarouna** and nearby is the **Monastery of Prophitis Elijah**. Two Byzantine churches, Agios Georgios and Agios Nikolaos are located in the village.

Soroni

The village of Soroni is located on the northwest coast, around 24kms from Rhodes Town. The village hosts a traditional festival to Saints Constantine and Helen in May each year. On 29 and 30 July, one of the most popular religious festivals on the island is held at the chapel of Aghios Soulas, which is located outside the village.

Soroni is also the location of the island's power station.

Beaches and resorts

Beaches and resorts

Symbols

⊕ Restaurant facilities
▮ Bars
◙ Water-sports
BF Blue flag beach *(International quality beach award)*

In 2019, Rhodes beaches were awarded 28 'Blue Flags', with the beaches within the region of Faliraki receiving the most awards. The criteria for a 'Blue Flag' award takes into account water quality, cleanliness, organisation, information, safety of bathers and the protection of the coastal environment.

A programme is in place to upgrade many of the island's beaches to make them accessible to the disabled. The plan is to include amongst a number of additions, decking to allow for easy access and specially designed changing rooms and toilets.

I have included all the main resorts and a broad sample of the many hundreds of beaches that exist on the island. But if you are adventurous, you may just find that hidden gem down one of the numerous tracks that lead down to the sea from the main coastal roads.

Please note that beach facilities can change without warning, the following are correct at the time of going to press. Also do not be confused by the different spelling of place names. As the Greek alphabet is completely different, the spelling of words can be translated a number of ways. The rule is, if it looks very similar, it is likely to be the same!

Rhodes Town beaches

Elli Beach BF ⊕ ▮ ◙

At the northern tip of Rhodes town is its most cosmopolitan beach and one of the most photographed in Greece. It is known as Elli Beach. The towering hotels and Aquarium stretch along the 400 metres of beach with row upon row of multi-coloured umbrellas.

Some sections of the beach are sand others are pebbles, but all have excellent facilities.

At the back of the beach there are bars catering for drinks and snacks, although in high season, it is sometimes difficult to find a sunbed as the beach fills up with the guests of the nearby hotels.

Further on there are the beaches of Akti Miaouli, Ixia and Ialysos. Both are well organised beaches composed of sand and pebbles. The sea tends to deepen quickly making them excellent for those who love to swim, but not good for families with young children. Due to the northerly winds which normally blow here they are also ideal for windsurfing.

Akti Miaouli ◍ ◙ ◪

Akti Miaouli is situated on the western side of the Aquarium peninsula, in easy reach of the town centre. Consisting of pebbles, the beach is well organised with sunbeds, showers and changing facilities.

It is mostly frequented by guests from the many hotels lining the promenade that runs along the beach.

Ixia ◍ ◙ ◪

Ixia is a cosmopolitan resort just 4km from Rhodes Town and the home of many of the island's luxury hotels. Therefore Ixia village which runs back from the seafront has all the facilities expected of a major resort.

Rather than just one beach, Ixia is a line of adjacent beaches, some public, but some private, which are owned and run by the hotels that front that part of the seafront. Those that are public are well organised with comprehensive water sports facilities, especially for surfing and windsurfing.

Along the esplanade behind the beach there are supermarkets, bakeries, patisseries and a wide variety of restaurants.

Ialysos ⏀ ◨ ◩

Ialysos is just 8km from Rhodes Town and is one of the most organised on the island. It runs parallel to the Avenue Iraklidon, the main west road out of town and where you will find some of the leading hotels based on Rhodes. The beach is ideal for surfing enthusiasts as it also tends to be very windy and consequently hosts a number of competitions such as the European Windsurfing Championships.

Beaches around the island (*clockwise from Rhodes Town*)

North east coast

Kalithea ▥ ◨ ⏀

Located in the north-east of the island, the beach at Kalithea is just 10km from Rhodes Town and is famous for its hot volcanic springs and the associated spa facilities built by the Italians in 1929 during their occupation of the island. However, the spa complex lay abandoned for many years until 2007, when after major restoration, it re-opened to the public as a venue for art and cultural exhibitions and concerts. Entry is 3€ between 08:00 and 20:00.

The area is characterised by a number of secluded small coves accessed by tracks lined with olive, palm and pine trees. They have sunbeds and are serviced by tavernas and bars.

The coves tend to be rocky both in and out of the sea, with many rock pools that make the area good for snorkelling, but not for paddling. However, in the same area are the sandy beaches of Reni and Kokkina.

Faliraki ⬛ ⓘ ❚ ⬛

Faliraki is the most developed and vibrant resort on the island, offering a wide range of amenities including a water park, a vast choice of water sports, restaurants, cafés and nightclubs. Situated 14km southeast of Rhodes Town and 10km from the airport, the resort extends for 5km south along the coast. As you enter from Rhodes Town, the first 3km of the resort are dominated by large hotel complexes built on the sea-front and opening directly onto the golden sand beach behind. The Falaraki area has become one of the main centres in the Aegean for Parasailing.

An official tourist information office is located in Faliraki Square, in the centre of town.

Tel.: *(0030)* 22410 85555

Kathara Beach ⓘ ❚ ⬛

Although ostensibly part of Faliraki, it is 3km further south from Faliraki's hotel complexes. Kathara comprises a sandy beach with some outcrops of rock and is well organised, offering a comprehensive range of beach facilities. Although next-door to its much more lively neighbour of Faliraki, it is a quieter more relaxed area, especially good for families. The picturesque bay has the small church of Aghioi Apostoloi (*St. Apostles*) and a small fishing harbour to explore.

Traganou Beach ⬛ ❚ ⓘ

Traganou Beach is a further kilometre south from Kathara and is composed mostly of small pebbles. This is an unspoilt beach with only a small section offering facilities such as sunbeds. It is mostly known for its impressive sea-cave and natural beauty. There is a small fish taverna serving the beach.

You can visit the Faliraki area by boat from Mandraki harbour in Rhodes Town.

Anthony Quinn Beach (*Vagies*) 🅱️ 🅣 ⓘ

Two kilometres further south, the first main beach you come to is Vagies Beach, better known as Anthony Quinn Beach. It was here and elsewhere on the island that scenes for the film **The Guns of Navarone** starring Anthony Quinn were shot. He was so enthralled by the beautiful landscape that after completion of the film, he purchased property in this area, which ever since has borne his name.

Vagies is a small beach sitting within a horseshoe shaped bay. The beach is approximately 200 metres long by 10 metres wide with fine sand, pebbles and rocks both in and out of the sea. It is a beautiful and peaceful setting, with pine trees growing down to the crystal clear waters, all adding to why the beach attracts so many visitors, both by land and sea. The beach is not serviced except for a few sunbeds and umbrellas and a small taverna above the beach. Families should be aware that the rocky shore can pose a danger for young children. There is a small jetty for boats, but there are no watersports available. The area is excellent for those who enjoy snorkelling.

Controversy still surrounds Anthony Quinn's connection with the area, as although he believed he had purchased the three plots of land needed to create his dream of "an international centre for artists and film-makers", the rights to the third plot, comprising the main beach itself, continues to be disputed by the Greek Government. After the actor's death in 2001, his widow Katherine Quinn has continued a legal battle to resolve the issue, taking the case as far as the Supreme Court.

Ladiko 🅣 ⓘ

In the next cove to the south is Ladiko Beach, one of the most beautiful beaches on Rhodes. The beach is composed of sand and pebbles, with lush vegetation extending down to the beach, giving rise to the emerald hue of its crystal clear waters and making it a favourite anchorage for the yachting fraternity. The organised area of the beach, with sunbeds and umbrellas, is situated on the left-hand side of the bay. Overlooking the bay perched on the cliff above is a taverna. The area is quite rocky, so it is not ideal for families with young children, but is recommended for snorkelling and sub-aqua. The beach is the busiest during the hotter months of the year, July and August, as the topography of the cove means that the water within this bay takes longer to warm.

Afandou ⷨ ⷧ ⷩ ⷪ

Afandou is the longest beach on Rhodes stretching 6km along the east coast and is situated 18km from Rhodes Town. The northern part of the beach offers almost no facilities, except a golf course at the northern end, but if you want to find a beach untouched by modern tourism, this area is for you. The beach is composed of sand and shingle, but shelves steeply into the sea, so not a good choice for families with young children.

As you travel south on the main road from Rhodes Town, you will see a large sign for Afandou Golf Beach. Turn left onto the beach access road and you will pass under a large concrete gateway. This is the route to the north end and quietest part of the beach. There are a few tavernas beside the long stretch of beach road running south, but if you intend to take advantage of this peaceful and at times deserted beach, it may be a good idea to also take your own refreshments.

Towards the end of the beach road, you will see a road on your right that leads to Afandou village. If you come to a dead end you have missed the turning! Take this road towards the village and then turn left onto the main road that runs parallel with the beach, look out for a sign for Sivilas Studios. At the sign turn left and this will take you down to Kolympia Beach.

Kolymbia Beach ⷨ ⷧ ⷩ ⷪ

Still really part of Afandou, Kolymbia is fully serviced due to the many hotels and apartments situated next to this southern end of the Afandou beach. There is a water sports centre called Antonis that offer a range of activities, including pedalos, canoeing, parasailing, jet skis and fly-fishing and in the nearby harbour there is a traditional taverna serving fresh seafood.

A mini train and bus service connect the village of Afandou with the beach.

Archangelos beaches ① ◼ ▨

There are four main beaches near and in easy reach of the town of Archangelos. In order running south they are Tsambika, Stegna, Agathi and Haraki, with Stegna being the nearest to the town.

Tsambika ① ◼

This is one of the prettiest beaches on the island with wide stretches of fine, golden sand and good beach facilities. Towering above the beach is the **Monastery of Panaghia Tsambika** perched on top of a rock outcrop at a height of 320 metres. You can visit the monastery from where there are magnificent views of the surrounding area. However, be warned, there are 297 steps to negotiate on the path that leads to the top.

The monastery is considered the island's protector and many of the locals are named after it, Tsambikos for men and Tsambika for women.

Stegna Beach ① ◼ ▨

Stegna Beach is ideal for all those looking for quiet as it has to be reached by a winding mountain road that descends from Archangelos down to the coast. On the road to the beach, are the caves of Koumellos, famous for its amazing stalactites and the recent discovery of objects from the Neolithic and the Mycenaean age. There is a tradition amongst the locals that the cave communicates with the sea. The cave is definitely worth a visit, but as it is usually locked, you may have to obtain the key from the Town Hall in Archangelos.

Stegna beach is composed of sand and pebbles with sunbeds and umbrellas for hire. A range of water sports are available and there are a number of tavernas directly behind the beach. A small picturesque harbour cuts the beach in two.

On the south of a large rocky promontory that juts into the sea lie the last two beaches of Agathi and Haraki.

Agathi ① ☎

Agathi Beach is only accessible via a dirt track from Haraki taking around 10 minutes to reach. Half way along this track is the beautiful medieval castle of **Feraklos** and well worth a stop to explore and take photos. Once you arrive at Agathi you will find a small secluded stretch of beautiful golden sand. The sea is shallow which is ideal for families and the less confident swimmer. Three small tavernas serve the beach and they also hire out sunbeds and umbrellas. Agathi is well known by the camping fraternity, as it has a cave at one end where one can bed down for the night. The beach and surrounding area is good for snorkelling.

Haraki (*Charaki*) ① ☎ ☒

Another idyllic small bay with a good range of tourist facilities and is popular with families, both local and from abroad. The beach is crescent shaped with the right-hand side composed of large pebbles whilst the left-hand side is of coarse sand. The beach here shelves quite steeply into the sea, unlike Agathi. The beach and surrounding bay is good for snorkelling.

Along the promenade there are mini-markets, cafés, tavernas and beach shops. The village is served by a regular bus service from Lindos and Rhodes Town.

Kalathos ☎ ① ☒

Kalathos is a long beach of some 4km, 7km north of Lindos. The beach consists of sand and small pebbles and shelves steeply into the sea. Parts of the beach are serviced with others left untouched by tourism. The beach never gets busy, even at the height of the season, so it is a good beach to chill out in peace. On the road that runs behind the beach there is a supermarket, a few tavernas and shops. Water sports are available on the beach.

Vlycha ⓘ 🔒 🔊

Vicha is a large beach 4km north of Lindos, consisting of golden sand with a gentle gradient into the sea. So large, it never feels overcrowded and is therefore a favourite with the local residents and those vacationing in Lindos. The right-hand side of the beach is the quietest, so a good choice for families with small children. Hotels dot the slopes behind the beach, with the largest in the centre of the seafront. There are sunbeds, tavernas, snack and café bars and a range of watersports.

Southeast coast

Lindos beaches

I cover Lindos and its attractions in the chapter on 'Villages'. With regard to beaches there, the picturesque area of Lindos is divided into three main beach areas. One on the north end of Lindos known as the Main or Lindos beach, one directly below the acropolis, accessed via Pallas Street in the town and known as Pallas Beach and Aghios Pavlos, south of the acropolis.

Lindos (*Main*) Beach ⓘ 🔒 🔊

The main beach at Lindos has the longest stretch of beach and is composed of sand. It has a gentle incline and remains shallow for some way out. It offers sunbeds and umbrellas, tavernas, changing facilities and pedalos. You can drive to the beach where there are several parking areas.

Pallas Beach ⓘ ▪ ▨

Pallas Beach is sandy with a shallow gradient and popular with the locals. Facilities are good with sunbeds and umbrellas, a good choice of tavernas, café bars, two supermarkets and changing facilities. A glass bottom boat operates hourly trips from both the jetty and Lindos beach and there is a watersports centre just beyond the jetty.

Aghios Pavlos (*St. Pauls Bay*) ⓘ ▪ ▨

Aghios Pavlos is situated south of Lindos acropolis and in an almost totally enclosed cove. It derives its name from the legend that St. Paul landed here in 51 AD, in order to preach Christianity to the locals. It is a picturesque bay with a little chapel on the cliffs and consists of two small stretches of beach. The larger, on the right, is a man made beach of golden sand that tends to get very busy in the high season with the sunbeds packed closely together. The second on the left is nestled amongst the rocks and is smaller, composed of sand and gravel. This beach has no sunbeds.

Rocks surround the cove making it an ideal spot for snorkelling. You can drive down to the cove, but you have to leave your vehicle well before you reach the beach, or alternatively you can walk down from Lindos. There are two small cafés above the beaches that serve food and drink.

All three Lindos beaches get very busy during the high season, so if you want a bit of peace and quiet these may not be for you.

Pefki (*Pefkos*) ⓘ ▪ ▨

Pefki Beach is often described as a further Lindos beach, but it lies 2km from Lindos on the south side of the Lindos peninsula overlooking Lardos Bay.

Pefki translated as 'pine tree' is one of the most famous tourist resorts of the island of Rhodes. It is a lively little resort with a long beach with good watersports, but doesn't suffer the overcrowding problems of the Lindos beaches. The beach is good for families with young children, being of soft sand and safely isolated from traffic.

Here you will find a quieter pace of life. However, Lindos is near enough for those who want a more lively night scene.

Pefki has several beaches of soft golden sand, which are bordered by pine trees, hence the resort's name. The main beach is wide enough to allow two rows of sunbeds and umbrellas. There are tavernas, several beach bars for snacks and watersport facilities.

Lardos ▦ ⓘ ▮ ▧ ▨

Lardos beach is composed of sand and pebbles, with crystal clear waters. Being one of the main beaches in the area it is well serviced with tavernas, snack bars, café bars, shops and supermarkets. The resort offers a good selection of attractions for all ages, with a wide range of watersports to choose from and a go-kart track behind the beach.

Glystra Beach ⓘ ▮ ▧

Glystra beach lies within a sheltered bay 3km from the village of Lardos and just 0.5km north of Katsouni Beach. A small and charming beach around 200m in length and 30m wide, with fine sand surrounded by attractive scenery. The beach tends to attract those who love quiet and calm. As it has a shallow incline, it is a recommended choice for families with young children. There is just one taverna/bar on the beach and there are canoes and pedalos to hire.

Katsouni ⓘ ▮ ▧

Katsouni beach is 1km long and is composed of golden sand with shallow waters, making it perfect for families with small children. It is a quiet and attractive little resort that is known as a haven for artists and photographers, especially at sunset.

There is a wide range of watersports available on the beach.

Kiotari ⚏ ⓘ ▮ ◈ ◂

Four kilometres further south is Kiotari, a modern cosmopolitan tourist resort along the length of an impressive, seemingly endless stretch of sandy beach. Holidaymakers here are usually families or couples looking for peace and tranquility, but with a good range of amenities. As you would expect with a modern resort, there are numerous beach, gift and souvenir shops that cater for all tourist needs. If you are just exploring the island, it is worth stopping off for a swim at this wonderful beach, or to refresh yourselves in one of the many tavernas or cafés. The beach has a wide range of watersports available.

Nearby in Asclipio is a Byzantine castle, worthy of a visit (*see page 61*).

Gennadi Beach ⓘ ▮ ◈

Genardi beach is composed of sand and small pebbles as far as the eye can see and is split into two areas, one organised and one untouched by tourism. The organised half of the beach has a wide range of amenities and there are numerous bars, cafés, tavernas and comprehensive watersport facilities.

The beach is surrounded by large hotel complexes, apartments, studios and shopping areas.

South coast

Prasonisi ⓘ ▮ ◈

At the southern tip of the island is the promontory and island of

Prasonisi. On either side of the 1000 metre sandy causeway that links the island with Rhodes are small bays. The landscape is amazing and the sea crystal clear. On the far south of the island is a lighthouse.

When the tide is high the island is cut off from Rhodes and can only be reached by swimming, but caution should be taken as there can be strong currents.

This area is a paradise for windsurfers and kite boarders, especially in July and August when strong winds generally blow. This is due to the fact that as long as the winds are strong, good windsurfing conditions are guaranteed on either the east or west side of the promontory. At this time of year the beaches usually throng with the camper vans and tents of the sporting enthusiasts.

There are mobile canteens on the beach, tavernas and shops nearby. For those who would like to stay there are also apartments and rooms to rent. Watersports rental companies and windsurfing schools are based in the area to cater for the experienced enthusiast, or just those wanting to try out one of the sports.

Northwest coast

Fourni ① ◨ ◪

Fourni is a small quiet beach with pebbles 3km from the village of Monolithos. It does not offer any facilities, so you will need to take your own basic needs. On this stretch of coast the sea is often rough, ideal for windsurfers and those who love authentic beauty. There is a path on the left side of the beach that leads to small secluded bays if you want to find total privacy. Sea Turtles (*Caretta caretta*) visit this beach to lay their eggs so you may be lucky and catch a glimpse of this wonderful creature.

Glyfada beach ⑩ 🔋

A short distance outside of Siana village is Glyfada beach, one of the less well known beaches on the island and ideal for those who enjoy exploring. Its many pine trees stretch down to the rocks along the coast and their reflection gives the waters a wonderful hue.

Kamiros Beach ⑩ 🔋

Kamiros is situated 50km from Rhodes Town and is composed of golden sand and shingle with some rocky areas and crystal clear water. It is not one of the more popular or busy beaches as there is no accommodation nearby, but it does offer the visitor a beautiful and peaceful place to relax. There are few facilities here although there are sunbeds and umbrellas to rent and one taverna on the beach.

Parking is available near to the beach.

In the nearby port of Skala Kamiros, fresh fish tavernas line the waterfront and from the harbour there are daily excursion boats that go to the island of Halki and the small islet of Alinda.

The important archaeological site of Ancient Kamiros is nearby and is recommended for a visit.

Activities for the very young

If you have booked hotel accommodation through a tour company, most offer activities for the very young within the hotel precincts and these should be listed in the company's brochure, or confirmed with the representative. However, other than the obvious days on the beach, I will outline a choice of activities that are suitable for children.

In or near most of the main resorts, you can usually find a limited number of fairground attractions for an evening treat, including dodgem rides, toy train rides and mini-carousels.

Boat trips around the island can be booked in most resorts, as can pedalo hire, banana rides and paragliding. The horse riding stables on the island also offer pony rides for the young. Both of these are described in more detail later in the chapter on 'Sports and recreation'.

Most of the larger supermarkets and souvenir shops stock a wide range of toys, including such things as childrens' fishing kits, snorkelling sets and fun beach items, such as bucket and spades, lilos, toy dinghies, frisbees, beach balls, racket ball sets, etc.

All the usual UK battery sizes are available in the supermarkets, but make sure the kids bring the battery chargers for their games consoles and equipment, or suffer the consequences!

The internet cafés on the island tend to attract the younger user and it may be an idea for them to bring any favourite computer game software with them, although most have games already loaded.

Water park

There is now only one water park on Rhodes, namely 'The Water Park' in Faliraki. This is a good venue for children, having a multitude of attractions, such as slides, water flumes and wave machines. Entrance fees are around 20€ for an adult and 15€ for children under 12. The entrance fee is for the whole day, so be prepared!

On site there are snack bars, bars and restaurants, but remember these extras can add quite a lot to the cost of the day. The opening hours are from 10:00 until 19:00.

Bars, clubs and adrenalin

Being the most popular tourist island of the Dodecanese, Rhodes, has a vast selection of nightlife. In Rhodes New Town, the hotel area between the streets of 28 Octovriou and Georgiou Papanikola bristles with bars and discos to suit all tastes. If you prefer seeing the night out in a more atmospheric setting, then the area of Odos Plantanos and Sokratous, in the Old Town, has a good selection of cafés and music bars, but as with the restaurants, they tend to be more expensive than those in the New Town.

Clubs

As good as the bar-life is, if you want to go clubbing, holidays on Rhodes will still live up to all your expectations. Bars are free to enter, but most clubs charge around 3 - 8€ entrance fee. Prices for drinks at the venues around the towns are quite reasonable, probably the same if not a little cheaper than back in the UK.

The most famous club on Rhodes is the **Paradiso Beach Club** on Kalithea Beach. Paradiso is an open-air venue with a 4,500 capacity and has an amazing sea view! Some of the most famous International DJs appear at the club. The music includes House, Tech, Electro, Progressive, Electronica & Mainstream.

Situated 4km from Rhodes Old Town, in Kalithea.

On the following pages, I have outlined some of the main clubs in Rhodes Town and around the island.

Rhodes Town

Angel Pure Club
The Angel Pure Club is situated in Rhodes Old Town on Dinokratous, just off the main Sokratous Street. The music is Club, Mainstream, Latin, Disco & Greek mainstream music.

Colorado Dance & Nightclub
The Colorado Dance Club is situated on Orfanidou Street, Rhodes New Town. The music is Mainstrean, House, Live Rock- Pop, R'n'B, Dance & Club music.

Elli Dance Club
Situated at the end of Mandraki Harbour, where Elli Beach starts, this club is the venue for International singers and bands as well as traditional Greek folk dancing. Elli is open every night until late and is free to enter.

Sticky Fingers
Situated on Anthoula Zervou 6, in Rhodes New Town (*behind the Blue Sky Hotel*). The music is Classic, Vintage, Hard and Modern Rock.

Todo Bien Coffee Bar (*Latin Bar*)
The theme behind the Todo Bien Coffee Bar is Latin, presenting the music and dance traditions of South America. Situated on Pithagora Street, in Rhodes Old Town.

Archangelos

Legend Music Club
Situated in Archangelos.

Ixia/Ialysos

Roi Mat Club Restaurant
Roi Mat Club is the new luxury club and restaurant situated on Iraklidon Avenue, Ixia/Ialysos. The club has an amazing view overlooking the sea. Music is Disco, Jazz, Soul, Funk and Greek mainstream.

Faliraki

Bedrock
Bedrock is one of the most popular clubs in Faliraki. It is a Karaoke, dance and cabaret venue. Before midnight, Bedrock's DJ's play a combination of soul, 70's, 80's and 90's music all the way up till today's chart toppers. After 12.30, Karaoke and dance become the theme with music ranging from indie to R'n'B.

Liquid Club
The Liquid Club opened in 2004 and is also situated in Faliraki. There are two floors to the club. The ground floor club offers Funky, Electro House, Trance and Old School House. The first floor is dedicated to R'n'B, Hip Hop, Garage and Charts.

Lindos

Amphitheatre Boutique Club
Situated in Lindos the open-air Amphitheatre Boutique was established in 1993 and has built a reputation as being one of the top clubs on the Greek islands. The club has a maximum capacity of around 2,000 and boasts amazing views of the village of Lindos and the ancient Acropolis.

Azzurro Club
The Azzurro Club is situated in Lindos and is open-air and on the road down to the main beach. The music is House, R'n'B, 80's, 90's & Mainstream.

Maritsa

Esperinos Bar/Club
Esperinos is situated in Maritsa village, 17km from Rhodes Town on the west coast. The music is Greek & Club music and every Friday there is a Karaoke party.

Open Wednesday to Saturday.

Adrenalin

There's so much to occupy you on Rhodes, so days can be as chilled out or action-packed as you like. For adrenalin junkies, don't miss the speedboat trips and loads of other exhilarating water and land-based activities that can be found in the main resorts. Alternatively there's the rare experience of standing inside the caldera of a dormant volcano on the island of Nisyros, or explore another culture by visiting Turkey.

Bungee Jumping

For those that don't suffer from vertigo, this is definitely an adrenalin-rush experience at 'New World Extreme Sports Company' based in Faliraki. To find the centre, just look for the tall orange towers near the beach.

Go-Karting

There are a number of Go-Kart circuits on the island, the two main ones are:-

Stan's Go-Karts, Falirakis. Tel.: 22410 86151, 14:00-23:00

Lardos Go-Karts, Lardos. Tel.: 22410 44510, 09.30 till late

Insider tip: If you want the track to yourself, then go in the morning or early afternoon, but if you want a more exciting atmosphere, then the evenings are best.

Jeep safari

You will find these advertised in the local travel agency offices. Dependent on the company, they either pick you up at your hotel, or from a convenient collection point. You will travel in a convoy of jeeps following an experienced guide over mountains, through forests and down dirt tracks to the coast. This is a great day out, taking in the lovely landscape of Rhodes and its villages. Lunch is organised along the route at either a taverna, or alternatively, a picnic or beach BBQ.

You can either be driven, or drive one of the jeeps yourself. To drive the jeep, a driver must be at least 23 years old and have held a driving license for more than 2 years.

Insider tip: Take plenty of suntan lotion and some good protective clothing, as with jeeps being open to the sun, you can come back looking like a lobster and don't forget to pack the driving licence!

Horse riding

For those who love horse riding, or want to try the experience there are there are two well organised stables on the island, both near to Rhodes Town. Both offer rides for beginners, which usually last for 90 minutes and cost around 30€. For the experienced rider, there are guided rides of around 3.5 hours exploring the beautiful forests and beaches and cost around 60€. Both stables have ponies available for young children.

Please contact the stables direct to confirm the rides that are available for your level of experience (*see page 153 for details*).

Scuba diving

There are five professional diving schools on the island, all but one based in Rhodes Town, although they all dive at various locations around the island, mostly in Kalithea Bay.

This is a wonderful sport, not only allowing you to view the beautiful marine-life in the seas around the island, but also to experience the amazing sensation of weightlessness. The centres offer dives for beginners, qualified divers as well as catering for snorkelling. Dives for beginners are organised in small groups for safety. The day usually includes all the training and one dive for about 30 minutes after which you can snorkel.

The diving session for beginners usually lasts 2-3 hours.

Extras services usually offered by the dive centres are pick-ups and drop-offs at your hotel and photos and videos of your dive (*see page 154 for details*).

Insider tip: *Items to take with you are water, towel, swim wear, camera, sun-hat and high-factor sun lotion.*

Water Park

The 'Water Park' is the largest in Europe, clean and well run and is located in the main resort of Faliraki. The entrance is at the top of a steep hill, but the park runs a free mini train to shuttle visitors from the main road to the entrance.

There are numerous rides throughout the extensive park including 'Thrill' rides, 'Multi' rides, 'Easy' rides and 'Kids Only' rides.

The park is fully staffed with 35 lifeguards. There are toilets, lockers, shower and changing facilities and a wide range of snack bars and cafés, with the food being of a high standard and moderately priced. All in all, the size and wide variety of rides within the park make it a fun day out for the whole family and as water parks go, it is reasonably priced.

Insider tip: *Take flip-flops or a pair of swim shoes to wear, as the ground and paved areas of the rides get baking hot and very slippery.*

Opening times: May, September and October, 09:30-18:00
Opening times: June, July, August and September, 09:30-19:00

Admission charge: 20€, children 3-12, 15€

Organised trips

Most tour companies will offer a selection of excursions to their customers at the traditional "Welcome Meeting". These range from the sometimes-abused title of a "Greek Night", day boat trips around the island including a barbeque, to more exotic options such as a trip to Marmaris in Turkey.

Many of the excursions can also be found independently, through the many tour companies situated in the towns on the island. Whilst the choice is down to the individual, before booking with your tour operator, I would recommend you shop around to see what offers are available and if possible talk to other holidaymakers who have already been on the tour in question.

The cost, especially for a family can be considerable. For example, a one-day tour of Marmaris with one of the major holiday companies for a family of 4, with two children under 12, will cost around 200€ and this does not include refreshments.

Symi

There are numerous organised boat trips to Symi as well as independent ways of visiting the island. As Symi is one of the main island destinations for day-trips, I have covered this in more detail on page 109.

Marmaris (*Turkey*)

This tour means an early morning start, usually being picked up from your hotel as around 07:00. The boat trip takes around 2 hours and you will have around 5 hours in Marmaris. However, most organised trips arrange visits to jewellery stores, leather works, or carpet shops, designed to part you from some more of that well earned cash. My advice is to ask what the tour includes before booking.

One "must do" during a visit, is to visit the bazaar (*meaning "place of prices"*), which is a fascinating experience, but just ignore the 'hard-sell' tactics and haggle hard before buying anything!

The boat returns to Rhodes around 18:30 and you will be coached to your hotel.

Insider tip: You need to take your passport and it is advisable to take Turkish currency if possible as the exchange rate can be poor once you arrive.

Day trips to nearby islands

There is a wide-range of boat trips on offer to the other main nearby islands of Halki, Tilos, Kos, Nisyros (*and its volcano*) and Kalymnos. Most depart from Rhodes Town or Kamiros. Detailed information can be obtained at the travel agencies in your resort.

For those who would prefer to go independently, on page 127, I have outlined details of the catamaran services from Rhodes to the other nearby island.

Coach tour of Rhodes

Rhodes has a wide range of attractions and amazing sites dotted around the island, so if it's not in your plans to hire a car during your stay, an alternative is to take an organised coach tour.

Both day and half-day tours are available which usually include Lindos, archaeological sites, villages and monasteries and include a tour guide.

Itineraries vary considerably from company to company and during the season, so my advice is to obtain details of the latest tours from the travel agencies in your resort.

Beach boat trips

From Rhodes Town and the main resorts you can take boat trips that will stop at a number of beautiful bays around the island. There are beach trips down the east coast which include a stop of around

3 hours in Lindos. The full day trips usually include a BBQ on board. The main companies offer a hotel pick up and return.

Insider tip: Take high factor sun lotion and a good pair of shoes, especially if the tour includes a stop at Lindos.

Sunset Cruise

If you are looking for a romantic start to an evening, you can take a sunset cruise from Mandraki Harbour to Kalithea and Faliraki. A number of boat companies in the harbour offer this trip, one being 'Sea Dreams'. There is usually a bar and music onboard. The cruises depart at around 19:00 and arrive back at 21:00.

Prices and times vary during the season.

Tony Oswin

Visiting Symi

Visiting Symi (*Simi*)

The day trip to Symi is highly recommended as the island is an attractive example of a small traditional Greek community. The majority of boat trips leave from Mandraki harbour in Rhodes Town between 09:00 and 10:30. Dependant on the company and the tour, the cost ranges from 18-25€. The trip to and from Symi takes around 2 hours each way and you dock back in Rhodes Town usually around 18:00-19:00.

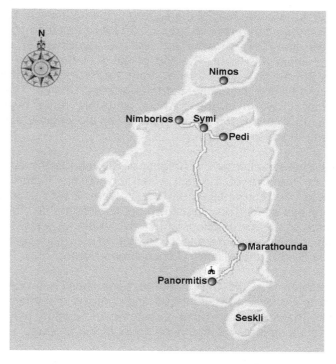

Symi is located 22km northwest of Rhodes and close to the coast of Turkey. The island is 14km north to south and 10km at its widest point, with an area of some 68 sq. km. The interior of the island is mountainous and quite barren. The main harbour and town is also named Symi and is divided into districts. Yialos (*Gialos*) is the main harbour area, Chorio (*meaning village*) is the top town. Pedi Bay is the area below Chorio, south of Yialos and Nimborios is the bay and settlement to the north of Yialos. The town nestles into the hillside overlooking the bay, with the houses painted in pastel colours and adorned with flowers of all colours. All this gives the impression that you are on a 'film-set', not in a real village! There are several smaller settlements around the island and a number of attractive beaches.

The Kali Strata is the main road that connects the harbour with Chorio. It starts at the rear of the square in the southwest corner of the harbour and comprises of around 350 steps that lead you up to the village area. On your way you will see attractive 19th century mansions lining the route. The top of the Kali Strata opens into Syllogos Square (a festival venue), from the back of which, a road leads round behind the castle and to Lemonitsa Church. There are spectacular views over the harbour and this route eventually connects up with the top of the Kataraktis, the original staircase connecting Yialos to Chorio.

The castle was rebuilt by the Knights of St. John in the early 15th century on the site of a much older fortification. It survived in reasonable condition until World War II, when it was used as an Axis munitions store. This was blown up, destroying the castle and the Church of the Assumption, which was within its walls. Parts of the walls remain and there is a plaque visible, commemorating Filibert de Niallac, the Knight's French Grand Master.

Symi Museum is in old Chorio and is signposted. It is open from Tuesday to Sunday, 10:00 to 14:00 and contains many interesting artefacts. Chatziagapitos House, a restored 18th century mansion is nearby and is open during the same hours as the museum.

The Monastery of Archangel Michael, located at Panormitis, is the island's most famous monastery. The original church of St. Michael was built around 450 AD on the site of an ancient temple to Apollo. It contains a splendid icon of the Archangel and two interesting museum sections.

Symi island thrived in the past due to the success of its sponge-diving fleet and boat-building industry. These reached their height during the second half of the 19th century, with the island's population rising to around 22,500. Today the population has declined dramatically to around 2,600, with tourism now being the main income for the islanders.

Most package holiday companies offer a trip to Symi on their itinerary, but if you are based in Rhodes Town or visiting, it is worth taking the time to ask for details from the various boat companies that line Mandraki Harbour, or have offices in Colona Harbour (*near the cruise ship port*). If you can't ask directly, then check prices and tour details being offered through your resort's travel agents, before making a decision on the trip that suits you. Organised tours from the other resorts on the island offer coach transfers to the boats based in Rhodes Town. Boats that offer trips to Symi include the Nikolias X, the Symi, and the Symi II. You will find the adv boards lining Mandraki Harbour, so you can easily find detailed information, times and prices.

Insider tip: The tour is not really suitable for very young children, due to the long boat journeys. However, if you want to visit the island independently, there is a quick catamaran service to the island (taking 50 minutes).

The main tour boats from Rhodes have an upper sun-deck and a lower air-conditioned cabin. They have snack bars which serve soft drinks, beer, coffee and light snacks and there are toilets on-board. English speaking guides usually accompany the tours.

Most tours allow you around three hours in the port of Symi to eat and explore at your own pace. There are a good selection of reasonably priced tavernas, cafés and bars in the town.

Tourist shops sell mostly sea sponges, leather goods, souvenirs and olive oil products. The shopkeepers are friendly and not 'pushy', unlike some in Rhodes Old Town! There is a horse drawn carriage tour in the town if you want to relax and chill out. The second half of the boat trip usually starts around 14:00.

Insider tip: Do not be late back to the boat, they leave promptly and if you are not there, the crew may presume you have fallen in love with the island and want to stay! There is usually a clock-face display sign next to the boat that confirms the time of departure.

The boat then sails to the south of Symi and stops for around an hour to allow for a visit the Monastery of Panormitos (*the second largest in the Aegean*), or for you to just explore on your own.

Finally the boat returns to Rhodes Town and if you are based in another resort and you have booked a full tour, a coach will be waiting to take you back to your hotel.

During the months of July to September the island hosts the Symi Festival.

Insider tip: It is worthwhile taking your swimming costume and a towel and if it's a breezy day, or at the beginning or end of the season, I would recommend taking something to keep the chill off during the journey back to Rhodes.

Getting around

For those who want the convenience, hiring a car is easy on Rhodes and the driving conditions are good. If you are on the island for more than one week, it may be worth hiring a car for only some of your stay as the island's bus services are pretty reliable, air-conditioned and regular. I have included bus information in a later chapter. Obviously this mode of transport is dependent on where you are staying and how accessible your hotel/apartment is to a local bus route.

Taxis are plentiful and in Rhodes Town, the largest of many taxi ranks is just outside the Old Town, on the harbour-front in Plateia Rimini. Tel: 22410 27666.

Rhodes taxi-drivers are expected to speak English, but the rule sometimes doesn't seem to be followed stringently. Taxi fares are fixed (*minimum charge 3.69€*), so to give you an idea of the cost, from Rhodes Town to Faliraki it will cost around 20€, to the airport the charge will be around 25€. Although taxi charges are fixed and the companies are very honest, it is always advisable to confirm the price of the journey before starting. The latest taxi prices can be found on the 'Rhodes Travel Info' page on our website.

If you decide to hire a car and you are travelling with a tour company, I am sure they will offer to arrange a hire car for you. Alternatively there is a broad range of small car hire companies on the island and my experience is that they are all of high quality and open to a little negotiation, especially at the beginning and end of the season. Mid season, you can budget on paying around 280 to 320€ for one week's hire of, for example, a Daewoo Matiz or equivalent, which includes air conditioning (*a must especially in the high season*) and power steering, with prices increasing to around 450 to 500€ for the top end specification of a jeep. However, take account of the fact that although a jeep is seen as more of a fun vehicle and will go where the lower slung 2WD cars won't, it is open to the sun which is nice at first, but you can return home looking like a beetroot! There is also nowhere to securely leave your valuables.

I am not being condescending, but remember to bring your driving licence with you, an obvious thing you may say, but you would be surprised how often people forget and can't hire a car. For non EU residents, you are required by law to have an *International Driving Licence*. The minimum age to hire a car is 23.

Seat belts are compulsory and children under 10 are not allowed to travel in the front of the car. "Drinking and Driving" is a serious offence with harsh penalties, whether you are on two wheels or four. Police roadblocks for breath-tests are a regular occurrence all year round, but especially in the summer months.

Also beware, if you park illegally the police will remove your registration plate and you will have to go and collect it from the police station, as well as of course, paying the appropriate fine.

When travelling around the island, please be careful when parking in the villages, the roads are very narrow and the local buses weave their way through with usually inches to spare between the bus and the buildings. You will therefore be in trouble if you block the road.

I would also recommend that you take note of the advice of the car company as to which roads your particular vehicle is insured for. Many of the un-metalled tracks on the island look fine as you enter them, but they usually get progressively worse, with large potholes and sometimes with nowhere to turn around. If you don't hire a 4x4 take care, or you may find yourself facing a hefty bill for any resulting damage to the car.

The main roads are good between the resorts, but on the minor roads and in the villages they can be potholed and uneven, so take extra care when exploring. Fuel is readily available with modern service stations throughout the island. The price per litre is on average around 1.80€ and that includes the personal service of an attendant filling the tank.

Scooter, motorbike, scooter, quad bike and buggy hire

Now we come to the hire of the two-wheel mode of transport. Although initially very attractive, especially to the younger visitor, as the cost is low and they seem fun, they are the most dangerous mode of transport. I have seen so many serious accidents involving motorbikes and scooters, resulting sadly in ruined holidays if not worse, that I would recommend anyone, young or old, to think again and if they can afford it, indulge themselves in the extra cost of a car.

Although all the hire companies supply crash helmets, most people you see on two wheels are dressed in shorts and T-shirts. The resulting injuries when flesh comes in contact with tarmac and gravel can be horrendous, even at low speeds.

If it's a more exciting mode of transport than a car that you desire and price is not a crucial consideration, then most motorbike rental shops offer 4 wheel quad bikes for hire. The daily hire charge is around 40€.

Also note though that most travel insurance companies now class quad bikes as a "dangerous sport" and do not cover their use. One unfortunate UK tourist to the island in 2011 was injured on a quad bike and had to be flown home. His insurers (*a quality company*) dismissed his claim and he was left with a bill for £14,000!

If it's a more exciting mode of transport than a car that you desire and price is not a crucial consideration, then most motorbike rental shops offer four-wheel quad bikes for hire. The daily hire charge is around 50€.

However, I believe a safer alternative to a quad is the 'new kid on the block', a buggy. Compared to quads they are much safer as their centre of gravity is lower and most models have a roll bar and safety belts as well as other extra features. Many hire companies are now offering this alternative to the quad and at a similar, if not the same, hire price.

With regard to pedal cycles, I have noticed a surprising number of visitors using this form of transport, although there are a lot of hills on Rhodes. For those who do enjoy cycling, I have included information on cycle hire in the chapter on *Sports and recreation*.

Finally, be careful whichever mode of transport you decide on, as the Highway Code is not stringently followed, especially at cross roads and with regard to "the right of way".

Bus information

There are two bus companies on the island, RODA and KTEL, both have their main termini in Rhodes New Town. Below I have listed the resorts and villages covered by both companies. I have also given an indication of price, but these can change during the season with no prior warning. The main terminus for the RODA bus company is the West Side Bus Terminus on Averof Street. The terminus for KTEL buses is the East Side Bus Terminus at Rimini Square. Both are near to each other at either end of Nea Agora Street. Rhodes City Line buses are run by RODA, but have a separate stop, situated along Mandraki promenade, across the street from the new market.

Tickets can also be bought on the bus from the conductor, or directly from the driver as you board. Keep your ticket whilst on the bus for confirmation of payment.

Bus stops around the island are marked by a sign, but you can flag down a bus away from these stops. Only some bus stops have the timetables displayed, and the buses are occasionally late. Also, note that most villages and resorts are serviced by both companies, with each company having its own bus stops. For example Faliraki has three, one along the main street, one at the town centre, and one right along the sea promenade, if you have a specific destination, confirm that the bus goes to your preferred stop.

RODA buses run routes around the town and also cover the west coast of the island, whilst KTEL buses take you everywhere else. Buses are frequent to the main resorts.

The ancient Acropolis situated just outside Rhodes Town centre, which includes the archaeological site of the Stadium, Odeum and Temples to Apollo and Zeus can be reached by RODA bus number 5 and costs 1.50€.

Municipal buses 'RODA'

RODA buses service Rhodes Town and its suburbs and include the following resort and village routes (prices are from Rhodes Town):- Paradissi and airport (*2.60€*)

Ialysos via Ixia (*2.30€*)
Falaraki via Kalithea (*2.40€*)
Butterfly Valley (*5.40€*)
Ancient Kamiros (*5.40€*)
Filerimos (*4.50€*)
Kremasti (*2.40€*)
Maritsa via Pastida (*2.30€*)
Theologos (*3.20€*)
Salakos (*4.50€*)
Kalavarda (*3.20€*)
Fanes (*3.00€*)
Damatria (*3.20€*)
Soroni (*3.00€*)
Embona (*5.20€*)
Platania via Apolonia, Dimilia and Eleousa (*4.50€*)
Skala Kamiros via Monolithos and Kritinia (*5.20€*)

RODA tel: 22410 26300/24129

'KTEL'

KTEL buses service the eastern areas of the island, which includes
the resorts and villages of (prices are from Rhodes Town):-

Lindos (*5.50€*)
Faliraki, via Kalithea (*2.40€*)
Tsampika Beach (*3.90€*)
Haraki (*4.90€*)
Stegna (*4.40€*)
Anthony Quinn via Ladiko (*2.40€*)
Kolymbia Beach (*3.90*)
Archangelos (*3.30€*)
Pefki (*6.00€*)
Gennardi via Kiotari (*7.10€*)
Kalithia (*2.40€*)
Massari via Malona (*4.10€*)
Lardos (*5.60€*)
Psinthos (*2.80€*)

There are KTEL bus services on certain days to Laerma, Katavia, Mesanagros, Vati, Profylia, Istrios, Arnitha, Apolakkia, Asklipio and Lahania. Please check with the bus company for schedules.

KTEL tel: 22410 27706/75134

KTEL and RODA bus timetables are available on our website on the 'Rhodes Travel Info' page.

Rhodes city bus tours

There are two companies that offer open-top bus tours of the city, the red and the yellow buses. They both offer 'hop on, hop off', which means that you can leave the bus anywhere during its route and resume the tour with a later bus.

Both tours take the same route which includes, the Old Town fortifications, New Marina, Acropolis, views from Monte Smith, Ixia, Grand Hotel, Aquarium and Mandraki Harbour.

I would recommend the tour as a way of getting a feel for Rhodes Town when you first arrive. If you have the time, you can stay on the bus for the whole tour and then decide when you will 'hop on' and 'hop off' on the next circuit.

You can join the busses anywhere along their route, but one of the best places is the terminus near the New Market, opposite Mandraki Harbour.

There is a 'plug-in' taped guide via earphones in English, Greek, French, Russian, Italian, Finnish and Czech.

Both companies charge 9€, children 5€ (*pay on the bus*)

Road Train City Tour

A road train called **'The Little Red Train'** offers city sightseeing tours from 09:00 to 21:00 (*high season*), 10:00 to 17:00 (*low season*), departing every hour (minimum 12 passengers). The tour

Tony Oswin

lasts for 45 minutes and covers the fortifications of the Medieval Town, the Temple of Apollo, the Ancient Stadium and the New Town centre.

The road train can be found outside the café Aktaion, opposite Mandraki harbour.

The cost is 7€. Children 3.50€ (*under 6's go free*)

(Prices are correct at the time of going to press)

Ferry and catamaran information

Rhodes to Marmaris

You can step into Asia for the day by taking the ferry to the bustling town of Marmaris, situated just across the straights from Rhodes. As far as tourist attractions go, there is little more than the castle and museum, but if shopping is your thing, then it is a good day out. You can haggle for carpets, leather goods, jewellery and *genuine* fake Rolex watches!

There are daily excursion boats to Marmaris leaving at 8:30 each morning that take around an hour to reach Marmaris, usually returning at 16:00 in the afternoon. You can obtain information and book tickets at one of the local travel agencies in the main towns, or at the port in Rhodes Town. The cost is 50€ p.p. (*90€ per couple*).

When you arrive at Marmaris port and disembark, if you want to do your own thing then don't bother with the tour bus that they shepherd you towards. Instead, go to the port exit where the yellow cabs are all lined up and jump in one, it's 8 euro to the bazaar. It is a good idea to visit the bazaar first before it gets too busy and too hot. Early on is also the best time to haggle prices down, as once the coach loads arrive, the store-keepers become less willing to reduce prices!

You will also find some quality shops just outside the covered bazaar around the area of fountain square. There are quality clothes, accessory and souvenir shops and although the prices are more fixed that inside the bazaar, they are still generally low. If you want lunch, or just a drink, walk from the square around to the harbour front and you will find some nice restaurants, just before you enter the main road. You will also find some nice cafés on Bar Street, a little cobbled road that runs parallel to the harbour front.

There is a duty free once you've gone through customs on your way back to the boat, where you will find such items as cigarettes are very competitively priced, but you are only allowed the normal customs allowance as you are outside the EU. Prices for spirits etc. are similar to those on Rhodes.

One word of warning, the queue at both the Rhodes and Turkish passport controls can be long and slow in the height of summer. So make sure you are at the ferry port early, as it can be nerve-racking realising your departure is in 5 minutes and you are still well down a very slow moving queue.

The ferry companies can offer a useful pick-up service when you book in advance. A minibus collects you from your accommodation, or a central pick-up point and takes you to the ferry port (*usually at no extra charge*).

Trips to the other islands of the Aegean

Daily ferry connections are available from Rhodes to Piraeus. The island is also linked with the main islands of the Aegean by ferry and catamaran services.

For those who would like to visit other nearby islands during their stay on Rhodes, the table below gives a 'guide' to the principle islands, the travel time, the time on the island and the cost of a return ticket.

I have chosen the services that allow you the maximum time to explore the particular island destination.

This information is for the catamaran services from Colona Harbour in Rhodes Town, which usually depart around 08:30, returning late afternoon.

Detailed information on the days of the services and times can be obtained from travel agencies in your resort, or the harbour.

Island	Travel time	Time on island	Price (Return)
Chalki	1hr 25mins	5.5 hrs	32€
Tilos	2hrs	5 hrs	35€
Nisyros	2hrs 50mins	3.5 hrs	39€
Kos	2hrs 10mins	5.5 hrs	60€
Kalymnos	2hrs 45mins	4.25 hrs	76€
Leros	3hrs 45mins	2.5 hrs	81€
Symi	50mins	8 hrs	32€

Eating and drinking

In this chapter I will first cover dining out. During the writing of this book I have meticulously sought to be unbiased and accurate with all the information I have included. However, where dining out is concerned, we have all had the disappointing experience of a poor meal in a highly recommended restaurant. Both differing tastes and changing circumstances can mean that a good restaurant to one person can be unacceptable to another. Also, as most restaurants on the island are seasonal, staff tend to move from one establishment to another, year to year and even during the season, which can affect the quality. Therefore in this chapter, I believe it is wise not to recommend any particular restaurants or tavernas on the island, but instead try to outline some basic information and useful hints.

The tips I would pass on are as follows:

First, if you are on a budget, be aware that the restaurants are more expensive in the main tourist areas such as Rhodes Old Town and Lindos. As Rhodes Town is the major tourist attraction, I will give an idea of the cost of dining there. In Rhodes Old Town, a meal for two with a mid-priced starter and main course and a glass of wine each, will be in the region of 50-60€. One of the most expensive meat dishes on most menus is steak, which is usually priced at 22-24€, with fresh fish similar in cost. Restaurants on Sokratous and the streets adjacent to it tend to be the most expensive, so by taking to the side streets away from the main tourist areas, you can save money. The restaurants in Rhodes New Town tend to be less expensive and there is a wide variety of choice, especially in the areas behind the large hotel complexes.

Out and about around the island, especially away from the main beach resorts, you will find lower prices in the restaurants and tavernas.

When choosing where you dine, it is usually the first impressions that count, is it clean and does it offer pleasant surroundings. However, a busy restaurant is invariably a good sign as is the appearance of the staff and the presentation of the menus. I certainly ask the locals, as they are more knowledgeable about the best eating-places in the area.

Insider tip: Don't go by the photographs of food outside the establishment, most are honest, but I had breakfast at a café bar in Rhodes Old Town and when it was served it bore no resemblance to the photo and the price was exorbitant. Just asking the waiter a few questions may save you a disappointing and costly meal!

Service in most of the restaurants is good, if sometimes a little slow, especially when it comes to obtaining the bill, but remember you are on holiday, so relax. It is acceptable for you to ask to look at the food in the kitchen and enquire about any particular dish. You may feel a little wary at doing so, but whenever I have asked, the staff have been more than happy to show me around and answer any questions. If you fancy fish, ask if it is fresh, by law they have to specify this.

Most dishes come with French fries and/or rice and often with a small amount of salad. If you are partial to salad, it may be advisable to order an extra portion, beware though they are usually large, so one will be ample for two people.

If, after your main course you do not order a pudding, many tavernas will bring some melon, mousse, or jelly on the house to thank you for your custom, or you will be offered a small glass of Ouzo or Metaxa. It is worth keeping an eye out to see what that particular taverna's approach is before ordering any dessert. One further point to remember is that in Greece the salt and pepper pots tend to be the opposite way round, i.e. the salt pot has multiple holes and the pepper a single hole.

Beware of ordering UK branded spirits or unusual liqueurs without asking the price first. On my first trip to Rhodes I ordered a malt whisky and almost had to take out a mortgage to pay for it!

Most tavernas and restaurants are open all day serving breakfast, lunch and dinner. For those who want a more British start to the day, a well-cooked and comprehensive English breakfast can be obtained at many tavernas, with only the bacon being a little different, but still very tasty. The cost with juice, tea or coffee, the usual egg, bacon, sausage, beans, tomatoes and toast is around 10€. The alternative of a continental breakfast is always available.

Lunch, if you can manage it after breakfast, is invariably from the same menu as that in the evenings, but most contain snacks and salads as lunchtime alternatives.

In the towns and larger villages, there are a number of fast food outlets, where you can eat in, or buy a take away such as a rotisserie chicken, kebab, or burger meal.

One word of warning though, in your accommodation, if you don't have a mini-stove in your room and the hotel/ apartments have a restaurant or bar-food facility, the management tend to frown upon guests eating their own food in the rooms. I would also advise that where it is acceptable, it is courteous to dispose of any food waste yourself and not leave it for the hotel cleaning staff.

Ouzeries

A traditional Greek style of eating out is at an Ouzerie, a blend of bar and taverna. Ouzeries usually only offer mezedes and possibly a few seasonal dishes, with (*if you want to be really Greek*) an Ouzo, Souma, or Retsina as an accompanying drink. Mezedes comprise a selection of small dishes or appetizers, placed on a platter or around the table for you to pick and choose.

Insider tip: *This is recommended as an easy and cost effective way to sample some unfamiliar Greek food.*

Tony Oswin

A quick guide to Greek food

For those less familiar with Greek food, on the following pages I have outlined the main dishes you will find in the majority of tavernas (*in alphabetical order*).

Appetisers

Briam (*also a main course*) - Briam is an oven roasted vegetable dish that can be adapted according to what is in season. Layers of vegetables are baked in a savoury tomato sauce and served either as the main meal or as a tasty side dish.

Dolmadakia - Vine leaves stuffed with rice and then rolled. A hot variation also contains minced meat. Served most often cold as an appetiser, but can also be served hot with an Avgolemono sauce on top. Its origin is thought to be from Thebes about the time of Alexander the Great.

Keftedes - Small rissoles or fritters, often made with minced lamb, pork or veal, onion, egg and herbs and sometimes with ouzo as a moistener. Keftedes are shaped into flattened balls and usually fried.

Mezes - A plate containing a selection of different appetisers, similar to the Spanish tapas, usually to be shared around the table. Mezes can include seafood, meats, vegetable dishes and dips.

Pitaroudia - one, if not the main traditional dish of Rhodes, are made from tomatoes, chickpeas, or minced meat and are fried.

Taramosalata - Greek caviar combined with breadcrumbs, oil, onion, and lemon juice to compliment any meal as an appetiser. This is a thick pink or white puree of fish roe (*dependent on the type of fish*).

Tzatziki - A yoghurt, cucumber and garlic dip to be served chilled on its own, or with pita or plain bread. Very tasty in a Gyro.

Main courses

Grilled meats - Grilled meat usually includes lamb chops, pork, veal and chicken, either plain or in a variety of sauces dependent on the restaurant.

Gyro - Thin slices of barbecued meat specially seasoned with herbs and spices, served with tomatoes and onions in a pita bread, and topped with Tzatziki. Best from a rotisserie.

Hilopites - Are a delicious kind of pasta, which is accompanied with tomato sauce or meat.

Kleftico or Klephtiko - Is a term that refers to any kind of meat dish that is sealed and baked. The word comes from the time of the Greek revolution, when bands of Greek guerrillas, called Klephts, hid in the mountains and cooked their dinner in pits sealed with mud, so that smoke and steam would not escape and betray their position. Usually it will be Lamb Kleftico that is on the menu.

Moussaka - A Greek national dish, Moussaka is prepared with sliced eggplant, lean ground beef, onions, tomatoes, butter, eggs, milk, cheese and seasonings and baked in an oven.

Omelette - Most tavernas offer a variety of omelettes on their menu.

Pastitsio - A Greek Lasagne combining macaroni, minced meat, cheese and covered with béchamel sauce.

Pilafi - Fluffy rice simmered in butter, spices and rich chicken stock.

Pizza - Where pizzas are concerned there are some tavernas that specialise, having the correct ovens and expertise. So my advice would be to ask around to find the best place to go, but personally I have found most are at least equivalent in quality to the best in the UK.

Roast Chicken - Both from an oven or a spit, cooked in olive oil. I personally think the rotisserie chickens are the best and taste as chicken should taste. Chicken in most restaurants on the island tends though to be in fillet form. However, there are a few tavernas where you can still get a half chicken on the bone.

Roast Lamb - Lamb prepared in the traditional Greek way, roasted with herbs and olive oil and often on a spit.

Seafood - As with the majority of Mediterranean countries, in Greece you can find a wide variety of fresh and tasty seafood. I would suggest though that before ordering you ask if the fish is fresh and not frozen. Many restaurants and tavernas have a chilled fresh seafood cabinet near the entrance and the waiters are usually happy to confirm the choice of fresh fish they have on offer.

If you order prawns, the average price is around 18€ and you get about six, king-sized and in their shells.

Souvlaki - Souvlaki are made from cubes of meat that have been marinated for several hours in olive oil, lemon juice & origano, then threaded on wooden skewers and grilled or barbequed. They can be beef, veal, chicken, lamb, or pork.

Spanakopitta - Spanakopitta is a spinach pie, about the size of a flan. These small pies are made with a spinach and feta cheese filling in filo-pastry. In Greek bakeries they are referred to as Spanakopittes, but don't be confused as they can also be called Spanakotiropitakia.

Stamnato - Usually made with lamb (*often spelt lamp or lab!*) with potatoes in tomato and garlic sauce, baked in a traditional pot called a Lamm.

Stifado - Stifado is a casserole made of beef, veal or lamb in wine with pearl onions, tomatoes, herbs and spices.

Patisseries

Baklava - Nut filled, paper-thin layers of glazed filo pastry soaked in pure honey make this the king of pastry desserts. Every country in the near-east claims baklava is its own.

Diples - Honey rolls so thin and flaky that they crumble when they are bitten.

Halva - Is a candy made from ground sesame seeds. It is an oriental originated sweet, but popular in Greece.

Kataifi - A delicious pastry made of shredded filo pastry rolled with nuts and honey and sprinkled with syrup. Found throughout the Mediterranean.

Koulouria - Also called Koulourakia - Breaded butter cookies with a light sugar glaze, perfect with coffee.

Kourabiedes - Sugar covered crescent shaped cakes that melt in your mouth. They are usually served at weddings, at Christmas, and on special occasions, such as birthdays and holidays.

Loukoumades - Feathery light honey tokens or sweet fritters, deep fried to a golden brown and dipped in boiling honey. A tasty delight from ancient Greece, where they were given as prizes to winners of athletic games.

Melomakarona - A honey cookie sprinkled with a spice-nut mixture.

Coffee

Greek style coffee - This is a thick, powdered coffee that is made in a brickee (*or brika*), which is traditionally a small brass pot with a long handle, though most brikas nowadays are made from stainless steel. This is not instant coffee, and even though powdered, the coffee used does not dissolve. The grounds settle to the bottom of the cup.

When you order coffee of any sort, you must specify plain, sweet or medium-sweet (*sketo, glyko or metrio in Greek, respectively*). You can also order Cappuccino, Expresso and other types of coffee in most restaurants. Tea is usually available, but it comes in a do-it yourself style and can taste a little odd due to the long-life milk often used. I would recommend you ask for fresh milk (*frésko gála*).

Shopping

Cigarettes, sweets and newspapers

In all the towns and resorts you will notice large wooden kiosks on the pavements of the main streets. This is where in Greece you traditionally buy such items as cigarettes and tobacco, newspapers, magazines, ice-cream, drinks, sweets and snacks such as crisps. The supermarkets also sell all of these except usually newspapers.

If you smoke and are visiting from an EU country, don't bother bringing any with you and remember Greece is in the EU, so you won't be able to purchase them in the duty free at your departure airport. Once in Greece you will find that they are vastly cheaper than back home, at around 4€ for a packet of 20. You needn't shop around as the price will be the same at all the outlets. All the main UK brands are available such as Marlboro, Rothmans, Superkings, Benson & Hedges, etc. As Greece is in the EU, the rule banning smoking in any enclosed building also applies here. In summer though, most tavernas and bars are open-air and therefore you are free to indulge.

For those who become homesick whilst away and want to know what new stealth taxes the government have imposed, English newspapers are available, although they will sometimes be the previous day's edition. I have personally seen on sale The Daily Mail, The Mirror, The Sun and a couple of the main broadsheets.

English magazines are rarer, but I have seen some of the main women's publications on the newsstands.

Our website has a link to all the main UK and US papers' websites and TV news reports.

Men's clothes and shoes

As with most products on Rhodes, clothes and shoes are on the whole cheaper than in the UK. However, the selection of modern men's wear is not as good as for females, but there are some good fashion shops in the larger resorts. There is a good selection of men's leather goods such as belts, bags and wallets especially in

Rhodes Old Town and the prices are reasonable, so you may be able to pick up a real bargain. Our website contains an International size conversion table on the 'Santorini Travel Info' page.

Insider tip: Some of the leather goods such as belts are reconstituted leather, which means that they don't last as long as solid leather, so ask if you want good quality.

Personal electronic items

I have yet to survey in detail the cost of personal electronic equipment, but my initial view is that it will be less expensive than in the UK and as Greece is in the European Union, it may be worth putting off that purchase and checking while you are over here. I will endeavour to check out this category of goods in the next month or so and add the results in the next update of this book.

However, it may be a problem if the goods turn out to be faulty. If you do intend to purchase expensive items, check first that the manufacturer's guarantee will cover the item back home.

Souvenirs

Well this is a difficult subject to write about as we all have a different view of what a good souvenir is. In all the resorts on the island there are a myriad of shops selling everything from quality items to the many explicit statues of well endowed male gods! Gold jewellery is good value as are leather goods and local pottery. If you really get stuck there is always a bottle of Ouzo, Metaxa or some local honey.

With regard to cosmetics, fashion, hairdressers and jewellery, I will pass this section over to my partner Carol.

Cosmetics

Although Rhodes is an island, as far as buying your moisturiser, body lotions, shampoos, make up etc and the all-important sunscreen you don't have to worry. Especially in the towns there is a good selection in the many pharmacies on the island and in some larger supermarkets. There are many known brands for sale but if yours is not available then there are equivalent Greek brands available at reasonable prices. In Rhodes New Town there are a number of large departmental stores and even a Marks & Spencer, all of which have an extensive range of perfumes, cosmetics and toiletries. So no need to waste valuable space and weight in your suitcase, just buy all you need when you arrive.

Fashion

Rhodes New Town has an array of different shops to cater for every taste, from fun boutiques, to designer outlets. On my first visit I made the mistake of buying my holiday clothes in the UK only to find that Rhodes New Town offered a good selection and in most cases a lot cheaper, with no compromise on quality. The range of beachwear and daywear available is extensive in most of the main resorts. In the New Town you will find most designer/ specialised clothes shops away from the main shopping precincts, down the many side streets, with shoes and handbags being especially good value.

Hairdressers

There are numerous salons in Rhodes New Town and most of the main resorts, and after a few days in the sun and sea, what better way to treat your hair, and yourself, than having a few hours relaxation and pampering. I have had personal experience of one of the salons in Rhodes New Town where I had an excellent shampoo, cut and blow dry for 40€ - extremely good value compared to UK prices!

Jewellery

It seems that nearly every shop you pass in Rhodes Town and the larger resorts sell some kind of jewellery including bangles, bracelets, rings, necklaces, earrings and much more. There is an amazing choice for every age and at modest prices. You could buy a different piece for each night of your holiday!

Supermarkets

The supermarkets in the resorts and main towns are well provisioned for the UK holidaymaker. Many brands are recognisable and if not, the supermarket staff are usually very helpful. Milk comes in cartons, just look out for the Greek word γαλα (*pronounced gàla*), the required percentage and skinned or semi-skimmed. Crisps are known as chips in Greece and chips are known as French Fries, although supermarket and taverna staff are familiar with both terminologies.

If you want to eat in, supermarkets usually have a good selection of fresh vegetables and fruit on sale, but meat, other than the basics such as cooked cold meats and bacon have to be bought from the local butcher, just ask and they will tell you where it is.

There are takeaways in the main resorts with a good selection of fastfood, also if you don't have the facilities to cook meat in your accommodation, many tavernas and restaurants, if you ask nicely, will do a takeaway service for main meat items such as a roast chicken.

If you want bread or pastries for later on in the day, I would advise you buy them early, as the supermarkets tend to sell out before lunchtime.

All the supermarkets sell wines and spirits, with again most of the brands we are used to in the UK available on the island. The selection of lagers is international, alternatively, the Greek lagers such as Fix and Mythos are in my view excellent. In addition to the supermarkets, there are usually dedicated off-licences in the main resorts that stock an even greater range. Prices are at least comparable with the UK, if not cheaper.

H.M. Customs

Regarding taking goods back home, if the goods you are carrying have had tax paid in Greece you do not have to pay any tax or duty on them in the UK. Any alcohol or tobacco you bring in must be for your own use and transported by you.

Own use includes goods for your own consumption and gifts. If you bring in goods for resale, or for any payment, even payment in kind, they are regarded as being for a commercial purpose.

With regards to quantities allowed, you are particularly likely to be asked questions by customs officers if you have more than:

800 cigarettes, 200 cigars, 400 cigarillos, 1 kg tobacco, 110 litres of beer, 90 litres of wine, 10 litres of spirits, 20 litres of fortified wine such as port or sherry.

Some goods are banned, such as plant materials that could contain diseases.

The information above is correct at the time of going to press.

With regard to buying honey as a souvenir or present, you may be told by some holiday reps that there are restrictions in taking it back into the UK. I have checked with H.M. Customs and DEFRA and as Greece is a member of the EU I can confirm there is no restriction.

The information above is correct at the time of going to press. It is not clear how Brexit will affect UK customs limits, but we will post information on our website when this is confirmed.

Please note: We review a wide range of holiday related products on our website in the 'Travel Tech' section.

Sports and recreation

Astronomy Cafe

The 'Astronomy Cafe', located at Profitis Amos, Faliraki, offers its customers the unique experience of viewing the cosmos whilst enjoying a relaxing evening drink.

Next to the cafe is the Hipparchos Observatory, which houses powerful astronomical telescopes, allowing cafe customers after dark the opportunity to view the moon, planets, nebulae, galaxies, and many other astronomical objects and learn about the cosmos in a fun and relaxed environment.

Tel.: (0030) 2241086112

Banana boats and ringos

For those not conversant with this activity, a banana boat is a long thin inflatable with seats for the participants positioned down its length. The banana is towed behind a speedboat and the objective is to stay on and enjoy the ride. Ringos are an alternative to the banana and are large inflatable rings towed behind the boat.

Banana and/or ringo rides can be found at all the main beaches. For safety's sake it is important that you wear the life jacket supplied.

Bowling

There is an eight lane ten-pin bowling alley at Kremasti, 8km from Rhodes Town. There are also pool tables, video games and a café.

Tel.: 22410 98233

Boat hire

Small outboard boats can be hired from some of the beaches on an hr/day basis (*approx. 10€/hour*). Larger sea going boats can be hired on the island on a daily or weekly basis. From Stegna Beach you can hire a motor boat for around 60€ for the day.

Cinema

Although not a sport, I have added the cinema here as a further entertainment for the visitor. There are two modern multiplex cinemas in the heart of Rhodes New Town, namely the Pallas and the Metropol Odeon. The Pallas Multiplex is located on Republic 13 Street and the Metropol is on Byron and Venetokleon, both are close to Diagoras Stadium. The cinemas show the latest international films in English with Greek subtitles, although animated movies are usually in Greek.

The Pallas, tel: 22410 70670
The Metropol Odeon, tel: 22410 28400

Cycling

Cycling is a popular sport on Rhodes, under Italian rule the residents of the island acquired a great love for competitive cycling which did not exist anywhere else in Greece.

A track was built at the Diagoras Municipal Stadium in 1930. Until 1984, the Rhodes cycling track was the only one available in Greece.

There are many routes for cycling in Rhodes but they are mainly concentrated on the mainland although they do exist in the South of Rhodes. The routes are on asphalt surfaces which are in good condition. National and International cycling competitions and events regularly take place on Rhodes, attracting many top riders.

The island offers many dedicated routes for cycling, but most are to be found in the southern part of the island. The routes are usually on good quality asphalt surfaces and offer a range of challenges to suit both the casual and sports cyclist.

The natural terrain of the paths and forest roads on the island also offer exciting routes for mountain biking.

Bicycles are available for hire in all the resorts and at low cost.

Fishing

Fishing is a popular pastime on the island for the locals, both by boat and off-shore, but for those visitors who would like to relax and try their luck with a rod and tackle, then most of the main resorts have a shop selling fishing tackle and bait.

It is often the local hardware retailer or similar, that doubles up as a fishing shop and although I am not an experienced fisherman, I have been surprised at the quality and range of gear on offer and the low cost of the items. To give an idea to the interested reader, a good extendable rod is around 20€.

The sea around the island abounds with a wide variety of fish, a fact that confirms the absence of pollution. The species include mullet, bream, blackfish, grey pandora, picarel and horse mackerel, with molluscs and crustaceans such as octopus and lobster.

Golf

The only 18 hole golf course on the island is Rodos Golf Club at Afandou (*Par 72*). Visitors are welcome, you can rent equipment, but the overall facilities are basic. The club plays host to a number of tournaments during the year.

From April to October, the cost of a round is 35€.
Tel.: 22410 51451

Horse riding

There are horse riding centres in the villages of Asgourou and Faliraki, both schools are fully licensed and provide lessons with good facilities and all the necessary safety equipment.

Experienced riders treck (*3.5 hours*) costs around 60€
A 90 minute beginners ride costs around 30€

Rhodes Horse Riding Club 'Kadmos'
Asgourou (*4km south of Rhodes Town*), Tel.: 22410 96651

Fivos Horse Riding Club
Faliraki. Tel.: 6938618252

Jet skis

Jet skis are available for hire on a number of beaches, these include Paradise, Kardamena and Kamari.

Paragliding

There is paragliding on most major beaches (*see the chapter on beaches*). All the major companies supply safety equipment.

Pedaloes and Oxoon

Pedaloes are self-explanatory and are available on all the main beaches. Oxoon are a recent addition to Rhodes and are motorised, joystick steered three-seat craft that look something like a dodgem car on the sea.

Spa and fitness

There are a number of the larger hotels on the island that have spas and gyms that are open to non-residents. My advice would be to ask locally where the nearest facilities are and check beforehand their availability and price.

Sub-aqua

There are five certified dive-centres on Rhodes, four are based in Rhodes Town and one in Pefki, near Lindos, they are:-

The Waterhoppers Diving School, Kritika, Rhodes Town. (*Padi 5 star*) Tel.: 22410 38146 (*also have an office in Lindos*)

Dive Med College, 45 Kritika, Rhodes Town. Tel 22410 61115 (*The Waterhoppers and Dive Med College work together*)

Trident Diving, Skevou and Zervou Streets, Rhodes Town. Tel: 22410 29160

Rodos Dive Centre, Rhodes Town. Tel.: 22410 20207

Lepia Dive Centre, Pefki, near Lindos. Tel.: 6937417970

All the dive centres offer introductory lessons for the beginner and full programmes for the experienced diver. Diving lessons for beginners usually last around 2-3 hours.

To give an idea of cost, a two dive inclusive trip will cost around 80€.

Insider tip: The best time to phone is between 17:00 and 23:00, after the boats have come back from a dive, or between 09:00 and 10:00 in the morning, before they depart.

Tennis, mini-golf, etc.

There are a vast array of other activities of the island, too many to mention here, such as tennis and mini-golf. My advice would be therefore to ask locally what is available and the quality of the venue.

Rhodes Tennis Club, Elli Beach, Rhodes Town. Tel.: 22410 25705

Windsurfing

Windsurfing is available on many of the larger beaches, but the best beaches are on the west of the island and at Prasonisi in the far south. There are two windsurfing schools for beginners.

Pro Center, Prasonisi. Tel.: 22410 91045

Money matters

There are branches of all main Greek banks in Rhodes Town. In Faliraki there are branches of the National Bank of Greece and Eurobank. In Ialisos there are branches of Alpha Bank, the Bank of the Dodecanese and Emporiki Bank. In Lindos there is a branch of the Emporiki Bank. At the airport, there are branches of the Emporiki bank. These all have ATM machines (*hole in the wall*), which take most debit and credit cards. Many stand-alone ATM's for the above banks are also situated within all the main resorts and in some major hotels.

Both Visa and MasterCard ATM locators can be found on our website. At the top of the homepage click the 'Travel Club' tab, then 'Travel Club Rhodes' and finally 'Rhodes Travel Info'.

The charges for the use of your card will for the most part depend on your bank back home, so it might be wise to have a discussion with your bank/building society before you leave and confirm the costs you will incur. If you use one of the banks on the island to exchange Sterling or traveller's cheques, take your passport with you to the bank to confirm your identity.

Other than the banks, there are a wide choice of exchange options, many hotels, shops and car hire companies will also exchange Sterling and Dollars, but make sure you check the rate and any charges first. Again the Greeks are very honest and I have never been short-changed, but it is advisable just to check.

In the banks, you may find a queue and remember life is at a slow pace in Greece. Look around as there may be a ticket-machine where you are required to take a numbered ticket identifying your place in the queue.

As to the exchange rate, I certainly have found that it is generally equal or better than that found back in the UK, so if you don't want the hassle of picking up currency before you leave home, just bring Sterling and change it on the island, for example in July 2019 the exchange rate in the UK was 1.22 on the island it was 1.24. The latest exchange rates can be found on our website on the 'Rhodes Travel Info' page.

Credit/Debit cards are accepted in most tavernas and larger shops on the island, but it is advisable to carry sufficient money with you on days and evenings out. One further point regarding drawing cash out abroad via a credit card (*learnt from personal experience*), is that many card companies will not only charge you a relatively high exchange commission, but also an additional cash advance fee. So if you want to use your credit card abroad, I would therefore I advise you check on potential charges before leaving home.

With regard to the safety of carrying money and leaving it in your room, as I have stressed before, the Greeks are extremely honest and over the last 30 years of travelling in Greece, I have never had anything stolen. On the contrary, I have accidentally left valuable items in public places, only to find them untouched hours later, but remember, there are not only Greeks on the island!

The bank opening hours are Monday to Friday: 08:00-14:00. However, if you are exchanging money, it is advisable to be at the bank well before 14:00.

Phone numbers: (*Prefix for Rhodes - 22410, required for all calls*)

Agricultural Bank of Greece	:	22410 21983/27810
Alpha Bank	:	22410 28951/31590
Emporiki Bank	:	22410 24201/23500
Eurobank	:	22410 77931/87001
National Bank of Greece	:	22410 35245/54000
Piraeus Bank	:	22410 76891/77893

Weather

What can you say about the weather on Rhodes other than it is invariably fabulous, with "wall to wall sunshine". What would be called summer weather back in the UK usually starts in May with temperatures rising throughout the following months (*see the table below*). Through late April and May, and then again in October, the weather can be compared to a good British summer.

The months of July and August tend to be the hottest, with average daily temperatures ranging from 91.4°F (*33°C*) during the day to 72°F (*22°C*) at night. The high temperatures often spark off thunderstorms in the evening, but these are not usually accompanied by rain and are more entertaining than a nuisance.

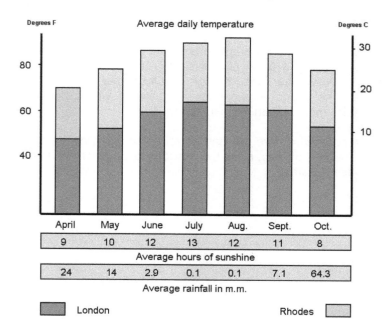

	April	May	June	July	Aug.	Sept.	Oct.
Average hours of sunshine	9	10	12	13	12	11	8
Average rainfall in m.m.	24	14	2.9	0.1	0.1	7.1	64.3

London ▨   Rhodes ▢

Rainfall is almost non-existent in summer, but showers can be expected between October and March, with the occasional heavier winter rain storm.

The Meltemi

The Meltemi (*the Greek equivalent of the French Mistral*) is a powerful wind that blows across all of the Aegean islands. It is the result of a high-pressure system over the Balkans and a low-pressure system over Turkey, creating strong northeast winds. The Meltemi occurs mainly during the summer with July and August being the worst affected months, but it can spring up occasionally in May and October. It usually starts in the early afternoon and can die out at sunset although occasionally, it will last through the night and repeat for three to six, sometimes even ten days. However, on Rhodes I have never found it a problem. Remember though not to leave valuables on the balcony, or you may return to find they've disappeared!

In October the evenings begin to cool, but that can be a blessing for those who enjoy a good night's sleep. Temperatures continue to drop into November and through to December. In January and February the island experiences its taste of winter, though this tends to be more like an English spring.

The latest weather forecast can be found on our website by going to the 'Travel Club' tab, open the 'Rhodes' drop-down menu and go to 'Rhodes Weather'.

Bugs, biters and things

This chapter is not for the paranoid, as I have been true to my word, adding a definitive list of the bugs and biters on the island. However, that does not mean that any of the following are a threat to life and limb and I can confirm that regarding all listed, I have never met anyone who has suffered more than the usual mosquito bites or the very rare wasp sting, so with that in mind, the facts are:-

Bees

Bees are less likely to sting than wasps, the reason being that the unlike the wasp, the bee stinger has barbs which prevents the insect withdrawing it. Brushing the bee off therefore results in the stinger and venom sack being ripped out of the insect, inevitably leading to its death.

Stingers should be scraped out sideways with a credit card, finger nail, or any sharp object. This helps to prevent squeezing the venom sack, which would lead to further venom being injected.

Treatment of the sting:-

1. Pull stinger out.
2. Cool compresses with ice.
3. Diphenhydramne (*Benadryl*) should be given to decrease minimal allergic reactions.
4. If a severe allergic reaction occurs, seek medical advice immediately.

Creams can be obtained from pharmacies to reduce the itching and inflammation.

Centipedes

Centipedes are not usually found in urban areas, they prefer rural and forested areas. Centipedes can bite humans, millipedes don't. The centipede's venom causes pain and swelling in the area of the bite, and may cause other reactions throughout the body. The majority of bites are not life-threatening to humans and present the greatest risk to children and those who develop allergic reactions. If bitten, consult a doctor or pharmacist at the earliest opportunity.

Hornets

There are hornets on Rhodes, but small numbers mean they are not a problem. They have a fearsome reputation for stinging and causing considerable harm, but in fact their stings are only a little more painful than that of a wasp or bee, due to the fact that hornet venom contains a larger amount (5%) of acetylcholine. Like most bees and wasps they usually only sting if you are blocking a flight path or are moving rapidly; however, nests should be avoided at all costs! For those that are not familiar with hornets, they have similar colouring to a wasp, being a member of the wasp family, but are twice the size.

Horse Flies

Found throughout warmer climates, the Horse Fly is the largest of the fly species. Recognised by its size and a grey mottling on the back of the thorax, only the female fly bites, just prior to egg-laying. If you do get bitten, make sure the fly is either swatted or gone, as they can be persistent little critters, drinking blood from the wound. Treat any wound as you would a mosquito bite.

Jellyfish stings

If you do experience a sting, the quickest remedy is applying urine to the affected area, so pick your holiday companions carefully!

Mosquitoes

There is the usual problem of mosquitoes on the island, but a good covering of mosquito repellent in the evenings, sold at all supermarkets, should generally protect you. It does though seem to be dependent on the person, I rarely get bitten, whereas my partner Carol seems to attract all the little critters. Her answer is she has better quality blood!

I would advise you to use a mosquito machine in your bedroom, which can be the old plug-in heated tablet type (*the tablets are still available*), or the new heated liquid system. After testing the latter, they are in my view superior, one bottle of liquid should last for the whole holiday and there are no fiddly tablets to change every day.

Mosquito bites

Although there are over the counter remedies available at the local pharmacies, you could try applying vinegar to the bites and you will find the itchiness will subside.

Poisonous caterpillar

In Greece, as in other Mediterranean countries, you will see white gossamer balls hanging from the pine trees on the island. **DO NOT TOUCH** either the nests, or any caterpillars that may be around. These are the nests of the caterpillar of the Pine Processionary Moth and can be very dangerous to humans and especially animals, as the hairs that cover their bodies are highly poisonous.

Scorpions

Rarely seen, the species found on Rhodes are *Euscorpius Germanus*, also called the Small Wood-scorpion and Mesobuthus gibbosus, known as the Yellow Scorpion. Both species are small at around 2 - 5cm. They tend to hide in crevices and such places as wood piles. In the most unlikely event that you are stung, the venom from both species is not life threatening. However, the advice is consult a doctor or pharmacist for treatment.

Sea Urchins

As with beaches anywhere in the world, sea urchins can be found in some beach areas on the island. If you have children, a quick chat at one of the beach tavernas, or a scan for their remains on the beach will confirm whether to take precautions. If they are around the simplest solution is to wear swim shoes when entering the sea.

If you do step on one, consult a doctor or pharmacist and they will advise you on the best course of action. However, don't worry, it will usually mean nothing more serious than a little discomfort for a day or two.

Here is the advice given in a medical journal:-

- Look for the signs and symptoms of a sea urchin sting: small spines embedded in the skin; a localized brownish-purple colour where the barbs made contact with the skin.
- Use sterile tweezers to remove any embedded spines.
- Control bleeding by applying direct pressure to the wound.
- Irrigate the wound with an irrigation syringe.
- Clean the wound with a disinfectant solution.
- Immerse the foot in hot water for at least 30 minutes, until pain subsides.
- Elevate the foot to control swelling.
- Dress the wound with a sterile bandage.
- Monitor for signs of infection. These signs include swelling, redness, pus, red lines radiating from the site of the wound, heat at the site of the wound, and fever.
- Seek medical advice.

Snakes

With regard to snakes, I have only seen one that was crossing the road and I saw it too late, it is now a flat-snake! There are a number of species on the island as in all of Greece, but only one is poisonous, namely the Viper. Most vipers are nocturnal and are only sporadically observed in the daylight, when they bask or mate. It is easy to distinguish a viper from the harmless species, based on their triangular head, swollen cheeks, stout body and a zig-zag pattern running down their back (*vipers are seldom longer than one metre*). A viper bite is not necessarily poisonous, in only about 30%

of bites there is actual injection of venom, and thus a need for anti-venom treatment.

The rule is if you see a snake, be on the safe-side and leave it well alone, but *please* be assured, it is extremely rare to hear of a bite. The precautions that can be taken are that when out walking in long grass, wear ankle length boots and do not turn large stones over, or place your hand into crevices that might be home to a snake. If you were to be the *one in a million* and are bitten, the advice is to be safe and seek medical help immediately.

Wasps

A more irritating insect can be the wasp. They tend to be found in greater numbers near the populated beaches where there is a good supply of tourist food, with the areas around towns and villages having very few if any. So it is dependent on where you are and what you are doing. I can honestly say don't worry, the locals don't, just try to ignore them. I certainly haven't been stung in five years of living in Greece and just find them irritating at times. Another answer is to buy a fly-swat and see how many you can exterminate. Sorry, I apologise to the entomologists amongst you.

If you find them irritating when you eating in a restaurant, ask the waiter for a "burner", usually a metal container filled with smouldering Greek coffee. The fumes are surprisingly an excellent deterrent to the little blighters. The good news is that come sundown they all return to their nest.

If you are unfortunate enough to get stung, the cheapest and quickest solution is to simply apply vinegar to the affected area. However, if you are allergic to stings, seek medical advice as soon as possible.

Creams to reduce the inflammation and itching can be purchased from pharmacies.

Health and Safety

Hospitals, doctors & community clinics

Whereas we all hope that nothing untoward happens on our holidays, especially health wise, as I can personally testify it sometimes does.

My view of the islands facilities is a good one, with all but the most serious incidents catered for on the island itself. In Rhodes New Town there is a General Hospital, well equipped and easy to find by following the signs in the town. There are also private doctors in Rhodes Town and most of the resorts. Normally the surgery is near the middle of the village or resort centre and can be recognised by a red cross on the door, or on a sign in front of the building.

There are 69 pharmacies in Rhodes Town and a total of 118 on the island, with at least one in each of the resorts. They operate on regular business hours (*usually 08:00 - 13:00 and 18:00 - 24:00*). One pharmacy in Rhodes New Town stays open during the night and the early morning hours. As this is organised on a rota system, you need to check locally for details. You can also be assured the quality of medicines and advice is equal to that back home.

For emergencies there is a twenty-four hour doctor service at the General Hospital in Rhodes Town. Alternatively there are private doctors you can visit if the need arises.

Remember, if you are an EU citizen, you should apply for a European Health Insurance Card (*EHIC*), now designated the A1 card. This will allow you to obtain free or reduced cost treatment abroad; this includes only treatment provided on the state scheme. The EHIC is free of charge and can be obtained within the UK in the following ways. I advise that you apply well in advance of your trip, as it can take a week or two for the card to arrive:

By internet at **www.ehic.org.uk**
By telephone on 0845 6062030
Or by form from the Post Office
(*For other EU citizens, search the web by entering EHIC*)

At the time of publication, it is not clear how Brexit will affect UK tourists regarding the A1 card and healthcare costs within Greece. We will be posting information on our website as the situation becomes clear.

Emergency contact details:

Rhodes General Hospital, located in Megavli, Rhodes New Town. Telephone: 22410 80100, Ambulance: 166

Emergency services, telephone: 112

Emergency Police :100

Dental services

My own personal experience of dental problems in Greece was in 2006, prior to moving to the island of Thassos to live. Only hours after arriving on the island, I was stricken by severe toothache and although I suffered for two further days (*I'm a man*), in the end I had to ask for help and was recommended to a dentist in Thassos Town.

All I can say is that I was amazed at the care shown to me on my arrival and the quality of the subsequent treatment. The surgery was modern, comfortable and very well equipped and the dentist friendly, he spoke fluent English and his chair-side manner was highly professional. I also found on my return to the UK, that the charges I had paid were less than half that I would have paid at home. All in all, I have to say that if I required dental work, I would prefer to have it done in Greece!

Common health problems

Stomach upset

If the worst happens, try adding a little fresh lemon juice to a Greek coffee and knock it back and in no time at all the symptoms will ease.

Sunburn

The most obvious advice anyone can give is to be extra careful for at least the first few days! If like most, you are not used to the Mediterranean sun, take it very easy and use plenty of high factor sun-block cream. You are especially vulnerable when there is a breeze, or when you are travelling in an open top car, a point I learnt from bitter experience, as you do not feel the full extent of your skin's reaction to the sun.

If the worst does happen, my first advice is to visit the local pharmacy and seek help. If this is not possible, a cold shower will initially relieve the pain, but drip dry, as using a towel will only aggravate the situation. For mild sunburn, cool compresses with equal parts of milk and water may suffice. Another remedy, recommended by many, is to spray or pat the affected areas with white or cider vinegar; this will relieve the pain and itching and hopefully give you a good night's sleep until you can visit a pharmacy.

The symptoms may also be relieved by taking aspirin or ibuprofen, but do not exceed the doses specified on the label.

(Our website contains a comprehensive 'Holiday Advice' section, with help regarding health issues).

Safety

Where safety is concerned, the subject falls into two categories.

First there is the safety aspect with regard to crime; one of the points that has always attracted me to Greece, especially the islands, is the low level of both property and personal crime. It does exist, or there wouldn't be police or prisons in Greece, but as far as the tourist is concerned it is rare on Rhodes. What property crime does exist tends to be from the less desirable tourists and criminals from the poorer states near to Greece. If you see the police on the island they will usually be drinking coffee or chatting to colleagues. But be warned, if you do transgress the rules, the police can be quite heavy handed.

The advice is of course be careful, however, I have accidentally left expensive items in public places in the past, only to return many hours later to find them just where I left them.

With regard to valuable items and money left in your accommodation, again I have never heard of any problems. The room cleaning staff, I have met in the past, have proved totally honest and as long as you lock the windows and doors you should have no need to worry. Sadly there have been a few incidents of cars being broken into, especially when the owners leave valuables on show. So the rule is when you leave the car, put valuables in the boot and it is also worthwhile leaving the glove compartment open and empty.

In the event of a loss of a valuable item, remember that if you are insured, your insurance company will need written confirmation that the loss was reported to the local police.

The second category is safety with respect to the activities you participate in during your stay. Safety in Greece is less stringently policed than in the UK, so when you are out and about, and especially with children, extra care should be taken. To give an example, some sections of the path and steps up to the acropolis in

Lindos have steep drops without railings and the cobbles have been worn so smooth you can easily slip.

Being abroad you should also take extra care when driving. Although the Greeks are mostly good drivers, compared to say the Italians, there does seem to be an unofficial rule that many follow, to the effect that they should not purely concentrate on driving their vehicle. Mobile phones, eating and drinking and even doing paperwork should all be a part of the driving experience!

Keep in mind though that if *you* are not experienced at driving on the right, mistakes can easily be made. It is a sobering sight on your travels, to see so many memorial boxes by the side of the road, especially by the cliff roads around the island.

As far as scooters and motorbikes are concerned, these are the most dangerous modes of transport on the island. You will see these being driven correctly with the riders wearing crash helmets, but usually only with shorts and T-shirts being worn and I have seen the damage tarmac and gravel can do to human flesh, even at slow speeds!

One further point is not to trust the zebra crossings, in Greece these mean little although the rules do give the pedestrian the right of way.

On the beach

If you have young children, just be a little careful on the beaches, as the currents can dredge out small holes in the seabed. This can be a shock to a child who finds that one minute they are in water a foot deep and the next up to their necks.

Swimming shoes

A recommended purchase is a pair of swimming shoes. They slip on and have a rubberised sole to protect you against sharp rocks and sea-urchins. They can be purchased at most beach-shops and cost around 10€.

Hints and tips

Batteries

All the usual UK battery sizes are available in the supermarkets at equivalent or cheaper prices than back home, but make sure you bring the battery chargers for your mobile phone, pda, etc.

Currency conversion

At the time of going to press, currency exchange rates were unstable and therefore I have not included a reliable rate in this edition. However, the latest exchange rates are available on our website at www.atoz-guides.com

Distance conversion

1 mile = 1.61 kilometres

Electricity

The electricity on Rhodes and throughout Greece is 220V and therefore compatible with UK equipment. You can purchase the two pin adaptors at most supermarkets. So if you do not already own one, it may be cheaper to purchase them on the island.

Electric razors

Some accommodation of the island have dedicated razor points in the bathrooms, but if not the adaptors sold on the island will take a twin pin razor plug.

Embassies telephone numbers

UK: 22410 22005
Italy: 22410 27342
Sweden: 22410 28816/24061
German: 22410 37125
France: 22410 22318
Denmark: 22410 94488
Holland: 22410 31571

Fire prevention

In the summer months, the vegetation on the island becomes parched and tinder dry. In the past the island has been ravaged by bush and forest fires and therefore it is essential to be careful, especially with discarded cigarettes. It is a strictly enforced law on the island that barbeques and camp fires are banned outside the town areas during the summer months unless clearly authorised.

Footwear

As I have mentioned elsewhere in the book, the vast majority of roads and alleyways in Rhodes Old Town and Lindos are cobbled. It is therefore advisable to wear good walking shoes when sightseeing, as the uneven surface can play havoc on the soles of your feet.

Google Earth

For those with web access, an interesting and informative site is:-

www.earth.google.com

Here you can view satellite images of Rhodes. You will need to download the free basic version software, but it is well worth it. For quick access to satellite images of Rhodes, add the following coordinates into the top left-hand corner box and press search. This will take you to Rhodes Old Town.

36 26 36 N, 28 13 38 E

Google Street View

In the last few years, the Google map car has been collecting data and photographs across the Greece to add the country to those already covered by their 'Google Street Maps'. For Rhodes, the main towns and tourist sites are now covered, To view 'Street Views', you need to enter 'Google Earth' and drag the orange man icon (*at the top right-hand side of the screen*) to the desired area.

Hair dryers

Many of the higher quality hotels and apartments supply a hairdryer in the room. If important, it is advisable to check with your tour-company or hotel before leaving home.

Internet café

Most hotels offer WiFi facilities to guests with their own laptops, tablets or smartphones and larger hotels usually have an Internet room. In the main towns and resorts on the island many of the bars and cafés now also offer free WiFi to their customers. Alternatively, tourist resorts usually have at least one Internet café, with the cost being around 3€ an hour, making it a cost effective way of contacting home and retrieving your emails. Remember though to take your important email addresses with you!

Mobile phones

Many mobile phone companies now offer reduced cost call packages for when you are abroad, but you will have to contact them and enquire what offers are available at the time of your trip. There are also companies specialising in offering cheap International mobile calls (*see our website for details*). Whichever alternative you decide on, remember to get your phone unblocked for international calling before you leave home.

Police

There are police stations in nearly every large village or town. You will recognize the police station by the Greek flag flying from the building and of course by the police vehicles parked outside.

On Rhodes there is also a tourist police service (*Touristiki Astinomia*) for more holiday related problems. You will find the office of the tourist police in the same building as the island police in Rhodes Town, directly on the harbour front.

The tourist police also supply information and brochures on the island and help in searching for accommodation.

Tourist police office Rhodes Town, tel: 22410 27423/23329

Post

As it is a tradition with us Brits to send home the usual wish you were here cards, I will cover posting on the island, but remember even if you post your cards soon after your arrival, it is highly likely you will be home before your cards!

The cost of the postcards and the stamps required for the UK is very low and you can purchase both in the supermarkets.

The Greek postal service is ELTA and post offices can be found in all the larger towns and are usually open from 07:30 to 14:00. Post boxes are coloured bright yellow and the post-office signs are yellow and blue.

Rhodes Airport

Sadly this information will only be of interest when you are returning home. However, the facilities are modern and as comfortable as any departure area. Once you pass through passport control, there are toilets, a café supplying drinks, snacks and chocolates and a small duty-free shop selling the usual cigarettes, booze and a selection of those last-minute present ideas.

Telephone: 22410 88700

Smoking ban

As in other EU countries, smoking inside public buildings, such as cafes, bars and restaurants is illegal and results in hefty fines, not only for the smoker, but also for the owner of the premises.

A further addition to the ruling became law in November 2019, banning people smoking in cars when children are present. The penalty for a passenger who is smoking is 1,500€, but if the driver is smoking, the fine increases to 3,000€!

Spelling

On your travels and in printed material, such as signs and menus, you will see names and places spelt in a variety of different ways. Do not be put off by the spelling, especially when you are trying to find somewhere, if it sounds the same, it probably is.

Sunbeds and parasols

If you are going to be a regular visit to the beach, rather than hire a parasol at an average of about 2.50€ a day, it may be cost-effective to buy one from one of the beachside supermarkets (*between 15 and 25€*). If you don't have a car and you are put off at the thought of carrying it back to your accommodation each day, you can ask nicely at the supermarket where you purchased it and they may allow you to leave it there overnight.

The same goes with the sunbeds; a good lilo can be purchased for around 15€ and gives you the added advantage of being able to use it in the sea, whereas a sunbed costs between 4 and 8€ each day. Many supermarkets have a compressor that they may allow you to use, so you can deflate it at the end of the day and take it back to your accommodation, or as before, ask nicely at the supermarket and they may allow you to leave it there.

Telephoning

Many apartments and hotels now have phones in the room; however, the cost of phoning home can be considerable. Alternatively many main landline providers in the UK, as well as independent telephone prefix companies, offer very low cost or even free international calls to Greece. It may therefore be cost effective to text relatives with your room telephone number and ask them to phone you. Remember Greece is 2 hours ahead of UK time.

Public telephones are to be found throughout the island, but remember, even in this age of mobile phones, there can be a queue of holidaymakers waiting to phone home, especially in resorts in the early evening.

To phone the UK the prefix is 0044 and you drop the first zero of the UK number, i.e. a London number that starts 020..... would translate into 0044 20....

To phone Greece from the UK and elsewhere, the prefix is 0030 and the prefix for Rhodes is 22410 (*the latter is required for all calls*).

One further option for phoning home is to use one of the many mobile phone/tablet aps that offer free, or low cost calls. Examples are Facebook, Google Voice, Rebtel, Skype, Vonage, Fring and Viber.

Tipping

Tipping is an awkward subject to cover as it is obviously dependent on the quality of service you have received and at your personal discretion. The service you will receive on Rhodes is usually very good and if you take an average price for a meal for two of 50€, a tip of 10 - 15% is not excessive and quite acceptable. The local wages are low and it may also be courteous and prudent to tip within these limits.

Toilet paper

A delicate subject, but an important one. Due to the small bore of waste pipes that are used in Greece, it is a rule that toilet paper is not flushed, but deposited in the bin by the toilet. Although this can be a little embarrassing for some, it is better than having to call on the manager of your accommodation to help unblock the toilet. Don't worry though, the bins are emptied on a daily basis and shouldn't cause a problem.

Tourist Information Offices

There are tourist information offices in both Rhodes Old and New Towns, Faliraki and at Lindos.

Useful telephone numbers

EU Emergency number 112

Greek national emergency numbers
Police: 100
Fire Service: 199
Medical emergency: 166
Coast Guard: 108

Tourist information: 22410 35945/44333/44335
Taxi station, Rhodes Town: 22410 69800
Disabled Taxi: 22410 69390
Port Authorities: 22410 27695

Water

The tap water on Rhodes is drinkable, as the island is self sufficient in fresh water. If you do have a preference for bottled water you can find it at all supermarkets, restaurants, cafeterias and kiosks. However, why incur the expense, it may even be bottled from local water.

Zebra crossings

One further point to remember is not to trust the zebra crossings, in Greece these mean little although the rules do give the pedestrian "the right of way".

For the very latest tips and information, please visit our website at:-

www.atoz-guides.com

Glossary of Greek words and phrases

Below, I have included a few useful words with their Greek counterparts. Although the majority of Greeks on the island speak some level of English, with many being fluent, I have found that the Rhodians really appreciate visitors attempting their language, even if you make a proverbial "pig's ear" of it!

Yes	Nay
No	Orhee
Good morning	Kalimaira
Good afternoon/evening	Kalispaira
Please	Parakalo
Thank you	Efkaristo
No, thank you	Okhee efkaristo
The bill please	To logargiasmo parakalo, or simply make a gesture in the air as though you were signing your name.....it works!
Hello/Goodbye (*singular/informal*)	Yiassou
Hello/Goodbye (*plural/formal*)	Yiassas
How much	Poso kani
Coffee	Kafé
Tea	Chi
OK	Endaksi

Where is	Pooh eenai
Do you speak English	Meelahteh ahnggleekah
I don't understand	Dhehn kahtahlahvehno
Can I have	Boro nah ehkho
Can we have	Boroomeh nah ehkhoomeh
I'd like	Thah eethehlah
Tomorrow	Avrio
Today	Seemaira
Toilets	To tooalettes
Wine	Krassi
Good	Kahloss
Bad	Kahkoss
Bank	Trapeeza
Police	Astinomeea
Doctor	Yatdros
Now	Tora
What is the time	Ti ora ine
Cheers	Yammas
Sorry/excuse me	Signomee

| Map of |
| **Rhodes New Town** |

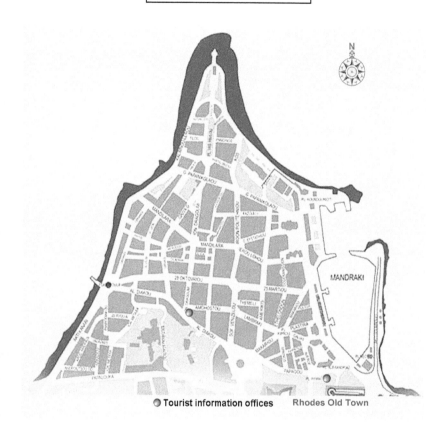

MANDRAKI

⦿ Tourist information offices   Rhodes Old Town

Tony Oswin

Map of
Rhodes Old Town

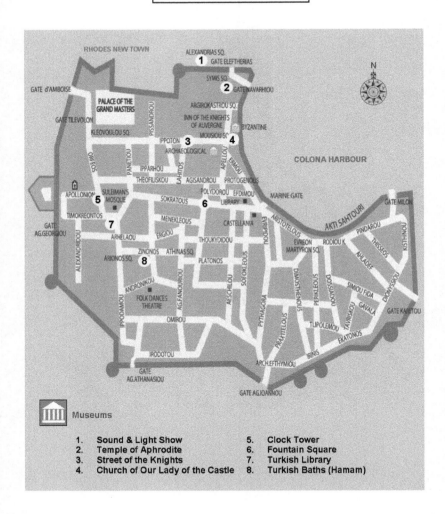

Museums

1.	Sound & Light Show	5.	Clock Tower
2.	Temple of Aphrodite	6.	Fountain Square
3.	Street of the Knights	7.	Turkish Library
4.	Church of Our Lady of the Castle	8.	Turkish Baths (Hamam)

Palace of the
Grand Masters

1. **Palace of the Grand Masters**
2. **Street of the Knights**
3. **Clock Tower**
4. **Mosque of Suleiman**
5. **Socratous Street**
6. **Turkish Library**

Map of **the Acropolis, Rhodes Town**

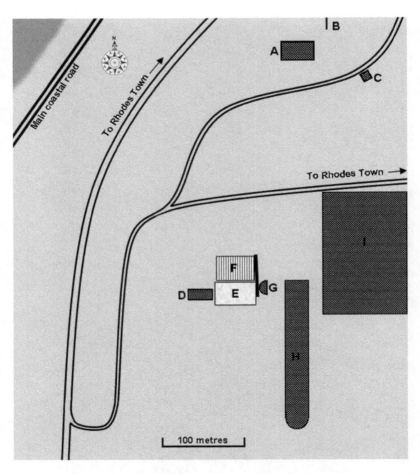

A.	Temple of Athena Polias and Zeus Polieus	F.	Sanctuaries, including the Artemision
B.	Stoa	G.	Odeum
C.	Nymphaea	H.	Stadium
D.	Temple of Pythian Apollo	I.	Gymnasium
E.	Terrace		

Attractions around the island

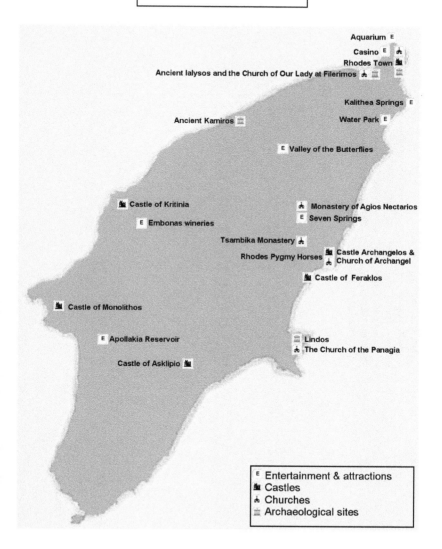

Aquarium E

Casino E ⚓

Rhodes Town 🏰

Ancient Ialysos and the Church of Our Lady at Filerimos ⚓ 🏛 🏛

Kalithea Springs E

Ancient Kamiros 🏛

Water Park E

E Valley of the Butterflies

🏰 Castle of Kritinia

⚓ Monastery of Agios Nectarios

E Embonas wineries

E Seven Springs

Tsambika Monastery ⚓

Rhodes Pygmy Horses

🏰 Castle Archangelos &

⚓ Church of Archangel

🏰 Castle of Feraklos

🏰 Castle of Monolithos

E Apollakia Reservoir

🏛 Lindos

⚓ The Church of the Panagia

Castle of Asklipio 🏰

E Entertainment & attractions

🏰 Castles

⚓ Churches

🏛 Archaeological sites

Tony Oswin

Map of **Ancient Kamiros**

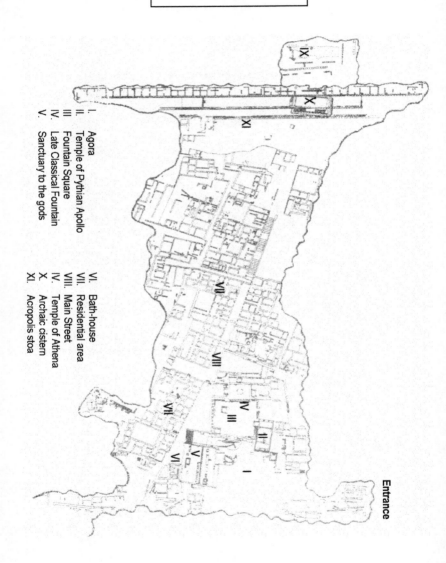

I. Agora
II. Temple of Pythian Apollo
III. Fountain Square
IV. Late Classical Fountain
V. Sanctuary to the gods

VI. Bath-house
VII. Residential area
VIII. Main Street
IV. Temple of Athena
X. Archaic cistern
XI. Acropolis stoa

Entrance

Map of Lindos

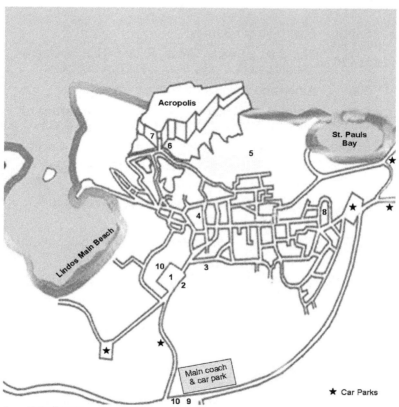

1. Main Square
2. Tourist Information Office
3. Post Office
4. Church Museum
5. Amphitheatre
6. Steps to the Acropolis
7. Rhodian trireme sculpture
8. Police station
9. Bus stop
10. Taxi stands

Greek timeline

Date	Event
776 B.C.	First Olympic Games
circa 750	The start of early Greek culture. Homer creates the epic stories "*The Iliad*" and "*The Odyssey*"
508	Athens becomes a democratic state
490 & 480	**Athenians defeat the Persians at the battles of Marathon (*490 B.C.*) and Salamis (*480 B.C.*)**
circa 450	Athens becomes a powerful state with an empire
472-410	Athens flourishes. Most of the famous Greek plays are written during this period
462-429	Pericles is General of the Greek army and is revered as a great leader
460-370	Hippocrates, the "father of medicine"
432	The Parthenon in Athens is completed
431-404	**The Peloponnesian Wars between Athens and Sparta**
404	**Sparta defeats Athens**
350	The Mausoleum is completed, a year after Queen Artemisia's death
338	King Philip of Macedonia takes control of Greece
336	Kind Philip is murdered, most likely by Alexander and his mother
332	**Alexander liberates Rhodes from the Persians**
336-323	Alexander conquers most of the known world, as far as India
146	Rome conquers Greece and subjugates it as part of the Roman Empire

Early Roman timeline

Date	Event
509 B.C.	Traditional founding of Roman Republic
396	Romans capture Estruscan city of Veii
390	Rome is sacked by the Gauls after its army is slaughtered at the river Allia
275	The Pharos lighthouse at Alexandria is finished
264-241	First Punic War
218-201	Second Punic War
216	At Cannae, Rome suffers its worst defeat to the Carthaginian Hannibal
202	**Hannibal is decisively defeated at Zama**
200-196	**Second Macedonian war**
192-188	**War with Antiochus III**
171-167	Third Macedonian war
149-146	Third Punic War
146	City of Carthage is destroyed
133	Tiberius Gracchus introduces novel reforms including land grants to the poor and food distribution; he is murdered
123	Gaius Gracchus, brother of Tiberius is also murdered after initiating reforms along the same lines
107	Gaius Marius is elected consul; begins major reforms of army
88	Rome grants citizenship to all free adult males in Italy
82	Sulla becomes dictator

77	Senate chooses Pompey to put down Sertorius's rebellious army in Spain
73	Uprising of slaves led by Spartacus
71	Crassus and Pompey defeat Spartacus
60	Pompey, Crassus and Caesar form the First Triumvirate
59	Caesar elected consul
58-51	Gallic Wars conquest of Gaul by Julius Caesar
53	Crassus dies at the battle of Carrhae
49	Caesar defeats Pompey at Ilerda in Spain. He crosses the Rubicon river; initiating civil war
48	At battle of Pharsalus Caesar defeats Pompey
46	Caesar becomes dictator
44	**Brutus, Cassius and other senators assassinate Caesar**
43	Octavian, Antony, and Lepidus form Second Triumvirate
42	Antony and Octavian defeat Brutus and Cassius at the battle of Philippi, destroying the last republican army
40	The Roman Senate makes Herod the Great King of Judea
33	Civil war between the armies of Octavian and Antony
31	Octavian crushes the naval forces of Antony and Cleopatra at the Battle of Actium
27 B.C.	Octavian takes the title of Imperator Caesar Augustus; the empire begins

Imperial Rome timeline

Date	Event
27-14 A.D.	Reign of Augustus as Emperor
9 A.D.	Three Roman legions annihilated by Germanic tribes at the Battle of the Teutoburg Forest
14-37	Reign of Tiberius
37-41	Reign of Caligula
41	The mad emperor Caligula is stabbed to death
41-54	Reign of Claudius
43	Claudius orders the invasion of Britain
54-68	Reign of Nero
64	Great fire in Rome. Persecution of Christians
66	Beginning of Jewish revolt
69	The Year of The Four Emperors
69-79	Reign of Vespasian
70	The city of Jerusalem is virtually wiped out by Titus
79-81	Reign of Titus
79	Eruption of Mt. Vesuvius; the twin cities of Pompeii and Herculaneum are buried in ash
80	Colosseum opens
81-96	Reign of Domitian
85	Agricola's campaigns in Britain end.
98-117	Reign of Trajan
101-106	Trajan conquers Dacia. Arabia becomes a province

112-113	Trajan's Forum and Column dedicated
115-117	Jewish revolt
132-135	Bar Cochba's revolt; final diaspora of the Jews. Hadrian's Villa built at Tivoli. Hadrian's Wall built in Britain
142	Wall of Antoninus Pius built north of Hadrian's Wall
162-178	Marcus Aurelius campaigns in Germanic Wars *(played by Richard Harris in the film Gladiator)*
180-192	The son of Marcus Aurelius, the egotistical Commodus is Emperor. In 192 his chief concubine has him murdered by strangulation
208-211	Severus campaigns in Britain. Arch of Septimius Severus erected
211 - 217	Caracalla is Roman Emperor
284-305	Diocletian's Reign
306-337	Constantine's Reign
312	The Emperor Constantine converts to Christianity. The Edict of Milan grants legal rights to Christians
325	The Council of Nicea - bishops agree the future of the Christian Church
330	Constantine declares Constantinople capital of a Christian Empire
circa 372	The Huns conquer the Ostrogoths
378	Battle of Adrianople, eastern Emperor Valens is killed by the Goths
379-395	Reign of Theodosius
395	Death of Theodosius I, final division into an Eastern and a Western Empire
396-398	The Visigoths ravage Greece

402	Ravenna becomes the capital of t Empire
410	Rome is sacked by the Visigoths
418	Visigoths settle in Aquitaine with capital at Toulouse
429	Vandals cross from Spain to Africa
436	Last Roman troops leave Britain
441	The Huns defeat the Romans at Naissus
circa 450	Beginning of Anglo-Saxon settlements in Britain
451	Aetius defeats Attila at the Catalaunian Plain
453	Council of Chalcedon: Constantinople wins ecclesiastical supremacy over Alexandria
455	Vandals sack Rome
476	Romulus Augustulus - last Emperor of the west is forced from his throne by the Germanic chieftain Odoacer, who is proclaimed King of Italy
532-537	Justinian builds the Church of Hagia Sophia
533-534	Re-conquest of North Africa from the Vandals
535-555	Re-conquest of Italy from the Goths
541-543	Great Plague
548	Death of the Empress Theodora
568	Lombards invade Italy
681	The First Bulgarian Empire is formed
690's	Muslims conquer Byzantine North Africa
717-718	Muslims lay siege to Constantinople
1453	Fall of Byzantine Empire when Turks capture Constantinople

Acknowledgements and websites of interest:

I would like to thank the following for their help in the writing of this book and the creation of the 'A to Z' website.

The Greek Ministry of Culture

The people of Rhodes

Isis Direct Travel

Olympic Car Hire

Design & Digital Creative by www.verkko.co.uk

For further information and the latest news from Rhodes, visit our website:-

www.atoz-guides.com

Your 'A to Z Travel Club' password:-

Salakos

2020

JANUARY

Mo	Tu	We	Th	Fr	Sa	Su
		1	2	3	4	5
6	7	8	9	10	11	12
13	14	15	16	17	18	19
20	21	22	23	24	25	26
27	28	29	30	31		

FEBRUARY

Mo	Tu	We	Th	Fr	Sa	Su
					1	2
3	4	5	6	7	8	9
10	11	12	13	14	15	16
17	18	19	20	21	22	23
24	25	26	27	28	29	

MARCH

Mo	Tu	We	Th	Fr	Sa	Su
						1
2	3	4	5	6	7	8
9	10	11	12	13	14	15
16	17	18	19	20	21	22
23	24	25	26	27	28	29
30	31					

APRIL

Mo	Tu	We	Th	Fr	Sa	Su
		1	2	3	4	5
6	7	8	9	10	11	12
13	14	15	16	17	18	19
20	21	22	23	24	25	26
27	28	29	30			

MAY

Mo	Tu	We	Th	Fr	Sa	Su
				1	2	3
4	5	6	7	8	9	10
11	12	13	14	15	16	17
18	19	20	21	22	23	24
25	26	27	28	29	30	31

JUNE

Mo	Tu	We	Th	Fr	Sa	Su
1	2	3	4	5	6	7
8	9	10	11	12	13	14
15	16	17	18	19	20	21
22	23	24	25	26	27	28
29	30					

JULY

Mo	Tu	We	Th	Fr	Sa	Su
		1	2	3	4	5
6	7	8	9	10	11	12
13	14	15	16	17	18	19
20	21	22	23	24	25	26
27	28	29	30	31		

AUGUST

Mo	Tu	We	Th	Fr	Sa	Su
					1	2
3	4	5	6	7	8	9
10	11	12	13	14	15	16
17	18	19	20	21	22	23
24	25	26	27	28	29	30
31						

SEPTEMBER

Mo	Tu	We	Th	Fr	Sa	Su
	1	2	3	4	5	6
7	8	9	10	11	12	13
14	15	16	17	18	19	20
21	22	23	24	25	26	27
28	29	30				

OCTOBER

Mo	Tu	We	Th	Fr	Sa	Su
			1	2	3	4
5	6	7	8	9	10	11
12	13	14	15	16	17	18
19	20	21	22	23	24	25
26	27	28	29	30	31	

NOVEMBER

Mo	Tu	We	Th	Fr	Sa	Su
						1
2	3	4	5	6	7	8
9	10	11	12	13	14	15
16	17	18	19	20	21	22
23	24	25	26	27	28	29
30						

DECEMBER

Mo	Tu	We	Th	Fr	Sa	Su
	1	2	3	4	5	6
7	8	9	10	11	12	13
14	15	16	17	18	19	20
21	22	23	24	25	26	27
28	29	30	31			

Test yourself on your Greek knowledge?

1. Which well known toy was invented by the ancient Greeks?

   ....

2. What is the ratio of tourists to Greeks during the summer months?

   ....

3. What is the official name of Greece?

   ....

4. How many Greek islands are there?

   ....

5. How many 'official' traditional dances are there across Greece?

   ....

6. On average how many days of the year are sunny in Greece?

   ....

7. Why are many roofs in Greece pained blue?

   ....

8. What is the population of Greece? 10.74 million

   ....

9. How many navigable rivers are there in Greece?

   ....

10. Which citizens are required by law to vote in Greece?

    ....

11. What commodity did ancient Greeks often buy their slaves with?

    ....

12. Who were not allowed to watch the ancient Olympic Games on penalty of death?

    ....

Answers on next page

1. The Yo-Yo

2. Three tourists to every one Greek

3. Hellenic Republic

4. 6,000 with 227 inhabited

5. 4,000

6. 250

7. To ward off evil

8. 10.74 million

9. None

10. ALL citizens above the age of 18

11. Salt, hence the saying "not worth his salt"!

12. Females

Notes

Lightning Source UK Ltd.
Milton Keynes UK
UKHW020650290720
367359UK00013B/1444